BASKETBALL'S ORIGINAL DYNASTY

The History of the

LAKERS

BASKETBALL'S ORIGINAL DYNASTY

The History of the

LAKERS

By Stew Thornley

NODIN PRESS

MINNEAPOLIS

ISBN 0-921714-39-7

Library of Congress Catalogue Card No. 89–92657

Nodin Press, a division of Micawber's, Inc.
525 North Third Street
Minneapolis, MN 55401

To Pa

Acknowledgements

Many thanks to:

The Lakers who took the time to share their stories and memories of the way it was: Vern Mikkelsen, George Mikan, Bud Grant, John Kundla, Jim Pollard, Howie Schultz, Dick Schnittker, Swede Carlson, and Tony Jaros, as well as Mrs. Ben Berger.

Harold Gifford, a copilot on Laker charter flights, for describing the details of a harrowing airplane trip with the Lakers in 1960.

George Rekela, my editor at Chapin Publishing, for reading the manuscript and making many useful comments and suggestions, and Donna "Scoop" Beckmann for her suggestions regarding the cover design.

My fellow members of the Society for American Baseball Research who turned out to know a lot about basketball as well: Alan Holst, Stan Carlson, Glenn Gostick, Bob Evans, Jim Wyman, Paul Rittenhouse, Joe O'Connell, Tom Jardine, Bob Tholkes, and Ken Ottoson.

Sid Hartman and Jay Weiner of the *Star Tribune, Newspaper of the Twin Cities*; John Duxbury of *The Sporting News*.

Tom Greenhoe of the University of Minnesota Sports Information Department and Dick Jonckowski, the voice of the Minnesota Gophers basketball team.

The Los Angeles Lakers' Public Relations Department.

Tim Bryant and Tim Leiweke of the Minnesota Timberwolves.

Wayne Patterson of the Naismith Memorial Basketball Hall of Fame.

League historian Bill Himmelman and Regina Flanagan of the National Basketball Association.

Sports Nostalgia Research of Tappan, New York and the Association of Retired Professional Basketball Personnel.

Bob Jansen of the *Star Tribune* photo library; Linda James and Don Church of the *St. Paul Pioneer Press-Dispatch* Photo Library.

Ted Hathaway of the Minneapolis Public Library.

John Baule of the Hennepin County Historical Society.

Tom Balcom of Mill City History Associates for his information on the history of the city of Minneapolis.

And my publisher, Norton Stillman of Nodin Press. This is the second book Norton and I have worked on together, and he has become a terrific mentor and friend.

Table of Contents

PROFESSIONAL
BASKETBALL

OSHKOSH ALL-STARS
1942 WORLD CHAMPIONS
—VS.—
SHEBOYGAN REDSKINS
1945 WESTERN DIV. CHAMPIONS

TONIGHT
MPLS. AUDITORIUM

SHEBOYGAN "REDSKINS"	OSHKOSH "ALL STARS"
1945 Western Division Champs	**1942 World Champs**
1. EDDIE DANCKER—All Pro Center —Nat'l.	1. DON SMITH—All Con.—Minn.
2. FRED LEWIS—All American—East Ky.	2. EDDIE RISKA—All Western—N. Dame
3. JAMIE DAWSON—All Con.—Texas A. & M.	3. GENE ENGLUND—All Am.—Wis.
4. AL. GRENERT—New York Univ.	4. RALPH VAUGH—All Am.—U.S.C.
5. MIKE NOVAK—Loyola Univ.	5. KENNY EXCEL—Uni. of Minn.
6. AL LUCAS—Fordham Univ.	6. JACK MADDOX—All Service—Quint.
7. KENNY SUESENS—Univ. of Iowa	7. CLINTON WAGER—St. Mary's
8. PAUL MAKI—Univ. of Minn.	8. BOB SULLIVAN—University Wis.
9. LUTHER HARRIS—So. Carolina	9. BOB CARPENTER—All Con., Texas
10. BOBBY HOLM—Seton Hall	10. LEROY EDWARDS—All Am.—Ky.

PRELIMINARY GAME STARTS 7 P.M.
MAIN ATTRACTION STARTS 8:30 P.M.
General Admission 60c incl. tax.

A 1946 game between Oshkosh and Sheboygan was played in Minneapolis to measure the local interest in professional basketball

The Stage Is Set for a Dynasty

Minneapolis, Minnesota in the mid-1940s was a typical Midwestern metropolis. The automobile and the coming of super-highways were hastening the migration of population and commerce to the city's outlying areas, but suburban sprawl had not yet set in.

Professional sports were a big part of the area's recreational scene. For baseball, Minneapolis had its Millers and St. Paul its Saints; each city also had a similarly named pro hockey team. Even though they were not major league, they still enjoyed a loyal, and rabid, following.

High-school sports filled in the gaps. And on the east bank of the Mississippi River at the University of Minnesota, Bernie Bierman, who had coached Gopher football teams to six Big Ten titles and five national championships in the thirties and early forties, had returned from the Marines and was at the helm again.

For the most part, Minneapolitans were enjoying the return to normal life following the end of World War II.

Some veterans were still taking advantage of an edict from Municipal Judge John Fineholt, who said he would "strike from the court tab drunkenness charges against discharged veterans, provided they have good service records." Fortunately, not all returning vets took the judge up on his offer.

For the past five years, newspapers had typically reported news like "YANKS LOSE 21 BOMBERS IN RAID ON GERMANY" and "8TH ARMY CLOSES TRAP ON NAZIS." Now, the headlines atop the *Minneapolis Tribune* trumpeted less dire happenings such as "Senate Rejects Meat Price Lid" and "Teachers Set Strike Deadline."

A headline on the front page of the December 1, 1946 *Minneapolis Tribune* read "Jane Russell wins London Battle of Bulging Bodice." Cleavaged well inside the sports section was a much smaller headline announcing "5,000 to See Pros Play Here." The Pros were two teams from the National Basketball League,

the Oshkosh All-Stars and the Sheboygan Redskins, who would be playing each other at the Minneapolis Auditorium that evening.

What were teams from two Wisconsin cities doing in Minneapolis? The reason for their appearance was the brainchild of an enterprising, twenty-six-year-old Minneapolis sportswriter, Sid Hartman. Hartman had convinced his friend Ben Berger, a local businessman who owned restaurants and movie theatres, to sponsor an NBL game to test the interest of Twin City fans toward professional basketball.

There would be local faces on the floor. The Oshkosh lineup included Don Smith and Kenny Exel, who both had starred at the University of Minnesota and Minneapolis Roosevelt High School. And the referees were two well-known coaches from the area: Frank Cleve of Minneapolis Henry High and John Kundla of St. Thomas College.

Beyond that, however, there would seem to have been little interest in the outcome of a game between two out-of-town teams. Even so, more than 5,500 people poured into the Minneapolis Auditorium that night to see Oshkosh beat Sheboygan, 56–42. (My folks, not yet married, were among the spectators. My dad could think of no better place to take a date than to a sporting event—a habit his son would acquire twenty-five years later—and he and my mom attended many basketball games together until September 11, 1948. On that day, shortly after saying "I do," my mom revealed the truth to my dad: she didn't even like basketball.)

The experiment of pro basketball was encouraging enough to prompt Sid Hartman to push for Berger to a acquire a team of his own for Minneapolis. In July 1947 Hartman accompanied Berger and Morris Chalfen, an ice-show promoter, on a shopping trip. With a check for $15,000 signed by the latter two, the trio purchased a basketball franchise, the Detroit Gems of the National Basketball League.

Major-league basketball was on its way to Minneapolis.

James Naismith

Basketball's Roots

Even though professional basketball in America had been around for a few years, in many ways it could be considered in its infancy at the time Minnesota was acquiring its first professional team.

During the previous two decades, the college game had blossomed as a gate attraction. But in basketball, as was the case with football at that time, the public considered the professionals to be distinctly less interesting than the collegians.

Nevertheless, professional basketball leagues had been in existence from shortly after the day in December 1891 when Dr. James Naismith had attached peach baskets at opposite ends of a gymnasium in the Springfield, Massachusetts YMCA.

Naismith's goal was nothing more than to provide an indoor athletic activity for his young men that was more enjoyable than calisthenics. He certainly did not envision the reception that would fall upon his new invention.

(How new this invention was became the subject of debate a few years later when archaeologists discovered that the ancient Mayan city of Chichen Itza in Yucatan had a walled-in "ball court." Beneath the stone grandstands, wall carvings depicted a sport in which seven-men teams shot a ball at vertical rings approximately twelve feet high. And according to *The Amazing Basketball Book*, there was another civilization that had practiced a form of the game: "The sixteenth-century Aztecs played a particularly tough brand of ball and hoop called *Ollamalitzli*. The player who made a shot was entitled to the clothing of all the spectators; the captain of the losing team often had his head chopped off.")

The stakes in Naismith's game were not as high, and it became an immediate hit with the participants; within three years, the game had been introduced nationwide. Rules and the style of play varied by geographic region, but for the most part, courts were sixty-by-forty feet and were enclosed by chicken-wire fences that served to keep the ball continuously

inbounds. These fences gave players the appearance of being caged in and led to a term still used today to describe basketball players, "cagers." The cages remained popular in the eastern United States into the 1920s.

There were many independent teams, but also early leagues, which were loosely structured and short-lived—the first being the six-team National League, which was formed in Philadelphia in 1898 and lasted six seasons.

Stronger teams, however, often found more success in barnstorming than in league play. The Original Celtics of New York (one of four teams enshrined in the Basketball Hall of Fame) won championships in various leagues, but they made more money by touring and playing local opponents.

Still, other leagues sprang up, all with essentially narrow geographic boundaries. One such organization was the American Basketball League, which was formed in 1925 by Joe Carr, who was also the president of the National Football League.

The early years of this period coincided with the "dance-hall" era of basketball. Eddie Gottlieb's Philadelphia Sphas (South Philadelphia Hebrew Association) played their ABL games at the Broadwood Hotel. Fans had to climb three flights of marble stairs to reach the ballroom, where every seat in the reserved section was individual, with plush green upholstery. The seating capacity at the Broadwood was 3,000, and there was dancing after the game. One of the Spha players, Gil Fitch, would exchange his jock strap for a cummerbund and, in a tuxedo, lead the band in the post-game fun.

Gottlieb contrasted this with the days when the Sphas played in a city league: "In one of those games, 1,700 people paid admission, but half of them never saw the game. They were standing on the long stairway leading down to the street, and all they got for their money was a relay of the score handed down from mouth to mouth."

A caged court at the Paterson, New Jersey Armory was
the site of American Basketball League games in the 1920s

The best professional team of the 1930s was the New York Rens, an independent all-black team named after the Renaissance Casino Ballroom in Harlem, which team founder Bob Douglas rented for their games.

Formed in 1922, the Rens would eventually succeed the Original Celtics as the kings of basketball. Competing against the best all-white clubs in existence, the Rens continued into the late forties and disbanded with a record of 2,588 wins and 529 losses (Two of their losses would come at the hands of the upstart Minneapolis Lakers.) The New York Rens, as a team, were inducted into the basketball Hall of Fame in 1963.

Another all-black team challenged the Rens' supremacy in the late thirties and early forties. The Harlem Globetrotters had played their first game in 1927; soon after, they gained notoriety by combining serious basketball with crowd-pleasing antics. The dazzling ball-handling displays and other "funny stuff" that would eventually become their trademark

was initiated as a means of providing themselves with a much-needed breather during games, while still keeping the crowd occupied.

But the Harlem Globetrotters' original intent was to become the world's best basketball team, not the world's funniest. In 1939 they received a berth in the World Professional Basketball Championships, an invitational tournament sponsored annually by the *Chicago Herald-American* newspaper. The Trotters made it to the championship game before losing to the New York Rens.

The Globetrotters were back again the following year and faced George Halas's Chicago Bruins team in the final game. Down 29–21 with five minutes to play, the Trotters battled back to win the game, 31–29, and earn the title of World Champions.

Professional leagues continued to spring up. The National Basketball League was formed in 1937. Over the next ten years, the NBL emerged as the best of the professional leagues in existence at that time.

The NBL had a heavy industrial connection; three corporations that fielded teams in the Midwest Industrial League combined with other business-sponsored teams to form the new league. The NBL was a group of "old pros" who attracted a devoted, albeit limited, number of fans to the high-school gyms and small auditoriums they used for their home courts.

The first NBL champions were the Akron Goodyear Wingfoots. Another company team, the Akron Firestone Non-Skids, won the title the next two years. The league left the scheduling to the individual teams and there was no uniformity as to the number of games each team played. In the league's first year the number ranged from nine to twenty.

One of the league's early teams was the Chicago Bruins, owned by a resourceful George Halas, who used two of his Chicago Bear football players as reserve forwards on the Bruins. Some of the league's early stars included an All-American from Purdue, John Wooden. Wooden played for the Whiting (Indiana) Ciesar All-Americans and would later go on to greater fame as the head coach at UCLA. He was voted into the Basketball Hall of Fame as a player in 1960 and as a coach in 1972, the only person to receive such dual honors.

Another standout was Oshkosh's six-four center Leroy (Cowboy) Edwards. Edwards had played one year at the University of Kentucky, but dropped out and joined the pros when he was told that colleges did not pay their players (at least not openly). With Oshkosh, the Cowboy led the NBL in scoring in its first season with a 16.2-points-per-game average.

In the beginning most of the players worked during the day and played for a team at night and on weekends. Over the years that changed and players could earn a fulltime living just playing basketball. Still, the new teams coming into the league continued to have a strong industrial connection.

The Chicago Gears were sponsored by the American Gear Company; Fred Zollner owned a piston-manufacturing company and a basketball team, the Fort Wayne Zollner Pistons. The Anderson Packers

The Harlem Globetrotters beat the Chicago Bruins to win the
1940 World Pro Basketball Tournament

13

were sponsored by the Duffey Packing Company

While the league was confined primarily to the Midwest and would embrace such hot spots as Anderson, Indiana; Flint, Michigan; and Moline, Illinois, its intense and successful pursuit of graduating collegiate stars led the NBL to much prominence.

Professional leagues were not the only attraction for college players at that time. Amateur Athletic Union teams were also in a period of intensive recruiting with offers of job security and immediate income that rivaled the pro salaries.

Bob "Foothills" Kurland, an All-American under Coach Hank Iba at Oklahoma A & M and a center whose dominance of that era was challenged only by DePaul's George Mikan, eschewed the pros and decided to sit behind a desk in Bartlesville, Oklahoma, home base for the Phillips Petroleum Company. Kurland also played for the Phillips Oilers basketball team.

Another All-American, Jim Pollard of Stanford, played for the Coast Guard and then a couple of other top-flight AAU teams, the San Diego Dons and the Oakland Bittners.

"Amateur" basketball was as much a way of life to Midwesterners as the college or pro game was to the city dwellers.

While the pros competed with the amateur leagues (which were often amateur in name only) for the top talent coming out of college, they competed with the colleges themselves for the fans and their entertainment dollars.

As interest in college basketball grew in the 1930s, a New York newspaper writer, Ned Irish, became convinced that the game could better be promoted in a large arena like Madison Square Garden. Irish was eminently successful in promoting doubleheaders at the Garden, and intersectional competition, sporadic up until then, became common as travel expenses and sizable guarantees could be offered to incoming teams. Rules, which varied between regions, became more standardized as teams from different conferences came together.

Propelled by the momentum Irish had created, the National Invitational Tournament (NIT) began in 1938 at Madison Square Garden. The next year the NCAA launched its own "official" championship tournament, but it would be at least a decade before it would surpass the NIT in prestige.

As college basketball thrived and AAU leagues also flourished, it hardly seemed that there would be

The battle of college basketball's two great giants: Bob Kurland of Oklahoma A & M and George Mikan of De Paul

room for another professional league in the mid-forties. But the end of the Second World War also brought with it the birth of many new enterprises. Waves of discharged veterans and a load of dollars flooded the market. The craving for entertainment, from a society that had been forced to practice austerity during the war, created never-before-seen demand in many areas. A second professional football league started in 1946, and that summer, another basketball league was formed. The Basketball Association of America was founded by arena owners in the Northeast looking for additional ways to fill their buildings. Most of the owners either owned or had ties to professional ice hockey teams, and to be their league president they chose Maurice Podoloff, who was the president of the American Hockey League. Of the moguls, only Ned Irish of the New York Knickerbockers and Eddie Gottlieb of the Philadelphia Warriors had notable backgrounds in basketball.

Maurice Podoloff

Other pro leagues still existed, but as they faded in prominence (the American Basketball League became a minor league and relegated its activities almost exclusively to weekend play), the Basketball Association of America and the National Basketball League had become the dominant pair – the older NBL with its star players, and the BAA with its large cities and arenas.

The upstart league did capture and produce some spectacular players and teams of its own. The Washington Capitols, coached by Arnold "Red" Auerbach, were led by North Carolina All-American center Horace "Bones" McKinney and produced the BAA's best regular-season record in 1946–47. But the first league championship went to Gottlieb's Warriors, who showcased one of the Association's first great stars, six-foot-five Kentuckian Joe Fulks, who averaged 23.2 points per game in a period when a single twenty-point game was considered sensational.

But the National Basketball League, although some of its lustre had faded, still had the best players, including a man named Mikan.

The Lakers' first coach—John Kundla

Three Years, Three Leagues, Three Championships

It was in this setting that Minneapolis found a team of its own.

For their $15,000, Ben Berger and Morris Chalfen returned from Detroit with little more than a few old basketballs, some useless uniforms, and a piece of paper saying they now owned a franchise in the National Basketball League. The Gems had been on the verge of collapse after having won only four of forty-four games the year before, and the NBL had already divided up the club and assigned the players to other teams in the league.

The start of the 1947–48 NBL season was less than three months away, and Berger and Chalfen were going to have to build from scratch. The first move they made was to hire Max Winter, a Minneapolis cafe owner and former fight manager, to run the operation and take a financial interest. The next step was to find a coach.

Joe Hutton, who had been at Hamline University in St. Paul since 1931 and had built the Pipers into a small-college power nationally, was first approached. But Hutton wasn't interested in making the switch to the uncertain professional ranks, and he turned down the offer. Hutton would continue at the helm at Hamline until 1965, would win a total of three National Association of Intercollegiate Basketball (NAIB) championships, and would compile a record of 591–208 in thirty-four years with the Pipers.

Instead, the Laker job went to thirty-one-year-old John Kundla, who immediately became the youngest coach in the league. Kundla left the security of his head coaching job at St. Thomas College in St. Paul only after receiving a three-year contract with the Lakers.

Born July 3, 1916 in Star Junction, Pennsylvania, John Kundla grew up in Minneapolis and attended Central High School. As a sophomore at the University of Minnesota, John was a member of the 1937 Gopher basketball team under coach Dave MacMil-

lan that tied for the Big Ten title (the Gophers last conference championship until 1972). Kundla also played baseball at Minnesota and, following graduation, he played one season of pro baseball with Paducah, Kentucky in the Class C Kitty League.

Kundla returned to Minnesota and served as an assistant to MacMillan, then took the head coaching job at DeLaSalle High School in Minneapolis and led the Islanders to the State Catholic Championship in 1944.

Kundla stayed active as a player as well during this time. In 1943 his team, the Rock Spring Sparklers of Shakopee, Minnesota, landed a berth in the World Pro Tournament in Chicago. Besides Kundla, the Sparklers roster had several other former University of Minnesota stars, including Clarence (Kleggie) Hermsen, Don Smith, Tony Jaros, Warren Ajax, Ken Exel, and Willie Warhol. The Sparklers won their first game before losing to the Washington (D.C.) Bears, an all-black team who went on to win the tournament.

A two-year stint in the Navy followed, and then Kundla took the coaching job at St. Thomas, where he produced an 11–11 record in 1946–47. When the Lakers called, Kundla, like Hutton, was wary, but he accepted the challenge and became the Lakers' first coach.

The Lakers still had no players until mid-August when they purchased Tony Jaros and Don "Swede" Carlson from the Chicago Stags of the BAA. Both men had been stars at the University of Minnesota and Minneapolis Edison High School before that.

Carlson was a member of the 1937 Edison team that won the state basketball tournament. In 1946–47 Swede had been the playmaker, defensive specialist, and Most Valuable Player on the Stags as he led them to a division championship and into the playoff finals against the Philadelphia Warriors. Carlson would play forward for the Lakers even though he was only six-foot-one.

The six-three Jaros, who could play forward or guard, graduated from Edison in 1940 and is still regarded as one of the greatest three-sport athletes in the history of the Minneapolis City Conference. On the basketball court, he set a galaxy of conference scoring records which stood until Jim McIntyre of Minneapolis Henry came along a few years later.

Jaros played baseball and basketball at the University of Minnesota until he enlisted in the Army. Following the war, Jaros signed a contract with the Minneapolis Millers and played three years of pro baseball. He also managed to fit in a professional basketball career in the off-season.

The real prize for the Lakers, though, came a few days later. A number of teams had been trying for years to sign Jim Pollard to a pro contract.

Pollard had been a star at Oakland Tech High School, and was a member of the Stanford University team that won the 1942 NCAA title. He left college to join the Coast Guard, and he played basketball for them for three years. From there, he joined the AAU ranks. Pollard had been turning down professional offers for years, as he had his eye on competing in the 1948 Olympics.

But Sid Hartman (who maintained an active role with the Lakers while continuing his duties at the *Minneapolis Tribune*), was able to persuade Pollard to forget about the Olympics and sign a contract with the Lakers. News of Pollard's signing even resulted in a phone call from Oakland mayor Joe Smith, pleading with him not to leave.

Because of the tremendous spring in his legs, Pollard was known as the Kangaroo Kid and was one of the few cagers in the country who could dunk a basketball.

At six-foot-five, Pollard became the tallest player on the Minneapolis team. The Lakers added another player of similar height, Bob Gerber, only days before their first game, but they were still searching for a big man when the season opened.

The Laker roster was loaded with Minnesota alumni. In addition to Jaros and Carlson, the team's opening-night lineup also had ex-Gophers Warren Ajax, Don Smith, and Ken Exel.

They were underdogs as they played their first game, November 1, 1947, on the road against the Oshkosh All-Stars. But the Lakers jumped to a fast start and held a 26–18 edge at the half. Minneapolis held the lead until an Oshkosh spurt tied the score at 47 with ten seconds left in the game. But in the final

seconds, Swede Carlson dropped a basket to give the Lakers a 49–47 win. Pollard had five field goals and led Minneapolis with ten points.

At this time, there were two pro basketball teams in the Twin Cities. The night before the Lakers debut, the St. Paul Saints, managed by Phil Gallivan and led by player-coach Bruce Hale, played their first home game in the newly-formed Professional Basketball League of America. The Saints lost to the Chicago Gears, 59–49, before 3,100 fans. (George Mikan was the game-high scorer for the Gears with seventeen points, although he was identified as George 'Hikan' in the *Minneapolis Tribune*. The *Tribune*, however, would learn how to spell his name correctly soon enough.)

The League of America had been organized by Maurice White, owner of the Chicago Gears. In fact, a syndicate headed by White owned all the teams in the new league. White handled all the salaries, transportation, and playing dates for the entire league. The League of America had sixteen teams and covered the midwest and southeast portions of the country, extending as far south as Houston, Texas and as far east as Atlanta, Georgia.

The team that gave the new league credibility and prestige was White's Chicago Gears. The Gears, who dropped out of the NBL after having won the league title the year before, were a gate attraction because of their center, the six-foot-nine All-American from DePaul, George Mikan. Mikan had averaged 16.5 points per game in his rookie season and was already considered the most awesome player in the pro ranks.

But Mikan and the Gears could not carry the load alone, and, after only two-and-a-half weeks, the League of America folded. The Chicago Gears immediately applied for readmission to the National Basketball League, but representatives of the remaining NBL teams unanimously rejected their application.

Players from the disbanded league became subject to a NBL draft. The Lakers, by virtue of having the worst record in the league the previous year as the Detroit Gems, were given the first choice. There was little suspense over whom they would pick.

George Mikan had grown up in Joliet, Illinois and studied for the priesthood in Chicago. Finally deciding he wasn't cut out to be a priest, George enrolled at DePaul University in Chicago.

In his freshman year, Mikan was invited to Notre Dame during the Christmas holidays to scrimmage

The starting lineup for the first game in the history of the Lakers:
Don Carlson, Bob Gerber, Jim Pollard, Bill Durkee, Don Smith

with the Irish basketball team. "They wanted me to run with the varsity, and I had a broken arch," recalled Mikan. "They kept throwing the ball at my feet, and, as a result, I kicked more three-pointers than any of your field-goal guys. (Notre Dame coach) George Keogan told me 'Go back to DePaul. You'll make a better scholar than a basketball player.'"

Back at DePaul, Mikan went to work on acquiring the skills that would eventually make him the most dominant player in the game (to the point that a few years later the marquee over Madison Square Garden would read 'GEORGE MIKAN VS. KNICKS').

Mikan credits DePaul coach Ray Meyer with his development. Meyer put George on a regimen to improve his quickness and coordination, with drills that included skipping rope, shadowboxing, and even ballet. And working with both his right and left hand, Mikan refined his soon-to-be famous hook shot. (John Kundla said it resembled more a "shot-put" than a hook shot.) Whatever it looked like, it made Mikan an All-American three years at DePaul and helped

him to lead the nation in scoring his junior and senior years.

George's greatest collegiate performance came his junior year when he led DePaul to the 1945 NIT title. In the semi-final game, DePaul beat Rhode Island State, 97–53, as Mikan matched the Rams' output by scoring fifty-three points, which was also a Madison Square Garden record.

The following year, Mikan signed a professional contract with the Chicago Gears as soon as the college season ended and he joined the Gears in time to compete in the 1946 Chicago World Professional Tournament. Even though the Gears only finished third, Mikan was named the tourney's Most Valuable Player as he averaged twenty points per game.

Less than a month into 1946–47 season, Mikan left the team in a dispute over his salary. He eventually returned to the Gears, but missed nineteen of the team's games. In the twenty-five games he did play, he averaged 16.5 points. He upped that average to 19.7 per game in the playoffs and helped the Gears

19

Mikan's first professional team was the Chicago American Gears. At George's left is his DePaul mentor, Ray Meyer, who also served as an advisory coach for the Gears. Although Mikan wore a jersey with the number 4 on it when he posed for this picture, his number throughout his college and professional career was 99. Mikan said he chose that number "because it was not quite a dollar."

capture their first National Basketball League championship.

With the Chicago Gears, Mikan began to revolutionize the game. Traditionally, guards and occasionally hot-shooting forwards had been the games' stars. Centers were there only to rebound; most were considered too awkward to shoot effectively. George changed all that. He was the first of the great big men, and he started a trend.

With the demise of the League of America, Mikan was momentarily a man without a team. The Lakers held his draft rights, but George had other options. He was receiving offers from independent teams, and, when he came to Minneapolis to discuss a possible contract with Max Winter, he was also pondering giving up basketball and completing his law studies.

The Lakers and Mikan were unable to come to terms, and George prepared to return to Chicago. But shrewd Sid Hartman, driving Mikan to the airport, "got lost" and Mikan missed his flight. Forced to

stayover in Minneapolis, George sat down with Winter again and finally signed a Laker contract.

The Minneapolis Lakers had found their big man. The acquisition of Mikan would also allow Pollard to move back to his normal forward position, after having ably filled in at the pivot in the team's first four games.

In addition to Mikan the Lakers also signed Jack Dwan of the disbanded St. Paul League of America team. Shortly after, they added six-foot guard Herm Schaefer, a veteran of the National Basketball League who had played with Fort Wayne and Indianapolis.

George Mikan scored sixteen points in his debut as the Lakers lost at Sheboygan, 56–41. Minneapolis had been 3–1 before Mikan joined them and dropped four of their first five games with him, but from there they won thirty-nine of their final fifty games to easily capture the Western Division title by thirteen games over the second-place Tri-Cities Blackhawks.

On January 18th, 1948 at Rochester, the Lakers

beat the Royals, 75–73. Mikan's basket with three seconds left broke a 73–73 tie and also gave George forty-one points, breaking by one the league's single-game scoring record, which had been set by Bob Carpenter of Oshkosh in 1946. Mikan played the whole game even though he was saddled with four fouls throughout the entire second half. (Only five fouls were needed for disqualification at that time as the games were only forty minutes long.)

Four nights later, in only his thirty-first game of the year, Mikan tied the single-season scoring mark of 632 points, set the year before by Al Cervi of Rochester. George would end the season with 1,195 points, nearly doubling the old record, averaging 21.3 points in fifty-six games.

With Mikan, the Lakers had the eyes of the professional basketball world on them; meanwhile, the world's funniest team, the Harlem Globetrotters, were feeling pressure from fans to show whether or not they were still the world's best team.

As a result, Lakers' General Manager Max Winter and Trotters' owner Abe Saperstein arranged for a game between the two teams to be played at Chicago Stadium February 19, 1948 as a preliminary to a Basketball Association of America game.

Chicago Stadium saw record attendance, as 17,823 fans watched the Lakers roar off to a fast start and carry a 32–23 lead into the locker room at the half. With a 103-game winning streak in danger of being snapped, the Globetrotters stuck to serious basketball and only once tried any antics, when they rolled the ball between a Lakers' legs to center Goose Tatum, who scooped it up and scored a basket.

Mikan was game high with twenty-four points and did an effective job bottling up Tatum, holding the Goose to nine. But with a minute-and-a-half left, the Trotters tied the score and got the ball back. Marques Haynes, easily acknowledged to be the world's greatest dribbler, kept the ball and dribbled down the clock until the final seconds when he flipped a pass to Ermer Robinson. As the buzzer sounded, Robinson unloaded a long set shot that went in. One timer said that Robinson had released his shot in time; another said he didn't. But the final ruling went against the Lakers and the Globetrotters had eked out a 61–59 win.

When the regular season ended, Minneapolis had a 43–17 record. The Rochester Royals, owned and coached by Les Harrison, finished at 44–16 to win the Eastern Division title by two games over the Anderson Packers.

Mikan was the overwhelming choice as the league's Most Valuable Player and was a unanimous choice on the NBL's All-Star team, along with Pollard, who was also named to the All-Rookie team. John Kundla finished second to Anderson's Murray Mendenhall in the Coach of the Year balloting.

Minneapolis defeated Oshkosh, three games to one, in the opening round of the playoffs, then swept Tri-Cities in two games in the semi-finals to advance to the championship round against an injury-riddled Rochester team.

It would be a classic matchup in styles: the brawny Lakers against the Royals, who depended on finesse. The strength of Rochester rested with their backcourt aces from Seton Hall, Bob Davies and Bobby Wanzer, with Red Holzman coming off the bench. In the middle was six-nine center Arnie Risen from Ohio State. Risen had averaged thirteen points per game during the season. But the Lakers would not have to worry about Risen; he had suffered a broken jaw and would miss the championship series.

The series with the Royals would be delayed, however, as the Lakers accepted an invitation to play in the World Professional Tournament in Chicago, which was in its tenth and final year.

The Lakers crushed the Wilkes-Barre Barons, who had been champions of the Eastern League (now the Continental Basketball Association) the year before, 98–48, in the opening round, and they squeaked by the Anderson Packers by three points in their second game. Their opponents in the title game would be a previous winner of the tournament, the New York Rens.

Led by Mikan, who set a tournament record with forty points, Minneapolis defeated the Rens, 75–71, to capture the World Pro Crown.

The Lakers had one day to rest before opening their best-of-five series with Rochester at the Minneapolis Armory (The Minneapolis Auditorium was under contract every spring for the Sportman's Show, and the Lakers had to find another floor for the playoffs).

The Armory was jammed to capacity as the Lakers took the first two games. The series shifted to Rochester for the remaining games, and the Royals stayed alive with a 74–60 win, despite thirty-two points by Mikan.

Mikan displays the trophy he received as the Most Valuable Player of the 1948 World Pro Tournament as he became the only two-time recipient of this award

In Game Four the Lakers, with no desire to face a do-or-die fifth game, grabbed an early lead and held it the entire game. Mikan scored twenty-seven and Pollard added nineteen as the Lakers, with a 75–65 win, took the National Basketball League championship in their first year in the league.

For the Lakers, however, their first year in the National Basketball League would also be their last. The Basketball Association of America had completed its second year of operations and continued to control the large population centers and big arenas.

But the teams in the NBL, particularly the Lakers, Royals, and the Fort Wayne Zollner Pistons, were more powerful than any in the BAA. BAA president Maurice Podoloff knew that, one way or another, the cream of the National League would have to be brought over to his Association.

Podoloff persuaded Rochester, Fort Wayne, and the Indianapolis Kautskys (who would change their name to the Jets) to jump to the BAA. The Lakers had little interest in making such a move originally, since they were on the verge of creating their own dynasty. But they decided if the other top NBL teams were going to break ranks, they would join them.

Clinging to life after the raid, the decimated National Basketball League tried to fill the gap by adding new teams, including a collection of New York Rens, past their prime, who formed a team representing Dayton. But the defections, and particularly the loss of top gate attractions like Mikan and Pollard, had left the NBL very close to death.

The Lakers would open their first season in the BAA with holdovers Pollard, Carlson, Mikan, Dwan, Jaros, Smith, and Johnny Jorgensen, a former teammate of Mikan's at DePaul. Newcomers Earl Gardner, a guard who had twice led the Indiana State Conference in scoring while playing for DePauw, and Mike Bloom, a former All-American at Temple who had averaged 10.6 points per game in the BAA the year before, would round out the opening-day lineup.

During the season Minneapolis would add to its roster Don Forman from New York University, Whitey Kachan of DePaul, and six-foot-four Arnie Ferrin.

Ferrin was a member of the "Blitz Kids" from the University of Utah, who found themselves fighting for the NCAA title in a strange way in 1944. Utah was defeated in the opening round of the NIT tourney in New York and was on its way home when they received word that Arkansas, on its way to the NCAA regionals in Kansas City, had been involved in a serious auto accident and had to withdraw from the tournament. Utah was asked to fill the Razorbacks' spot. Since Kansas City was on the way home, Utah accepted.

With a freshman-dominated squad averaging 18 1/2 years of age, Utah defeated Missouri and Iowa State to win the regional. They then headed back to New York for the championship game, and, behind Ferrin's twenty-two points, defeated Dartmouth,

1947–48 NATIONAL BASKETBALL LEAGUE CHAMPIONS
Herm Schaefer, Don Carlson, Paul Napolitano, Tony Jaros, Don Smith, Johnny Jorgensen, Jack Dwan, Jim Pollard, George Mikan

42–40, to win the NCAA championship. Ferrin was voted the tournament's Most Valuable Player.

The Lakers opened the 1948–49 season in Baltimore against the defending BAA-champion Bullets. Herm Schaefer led the way with twenty-three points as the Lakers won, 84–72.

Of the old BAA clubs, only Washington appeared to be in the Lakers' class. The Capitols were coached by Red Auerbach. With six-nine Bones McKinney at center and a backcourt consisting of Bob Feerick, a superb ball-handler, and hot-shooting Fred Scolari, the Caps won their first thirteen games to open a big lead in the Eastern Division. Meanwhile, the Lakers fought with Rochester and the St. Louis Bombers for the top spot in the Western Division in the early part of the season.

On November 24, Minneapolis set a single-game league scoring record when they defeated the Providence Steamrollers, 117–89. A few weeks later, Mikan scored forty-seven points in a game to tie another BAA mark. On January 30, 1949, George scored forty-eight to set a new record. That record was short-lived, however, as less than a fortnight later, Philadelphia's Joe Fulks scored sixty-three points in one game.

Fulks and Mikan battled the rest of the season for the scoring lead, with Mikan emerging as the league champion with 28.3 points per game. Seven times during the season Mikan scored more than forty points in a game. Twice he topped fifty.

As for the team, the Lakers were unable to shake Rochester, their old nemesis from the National League. Minneapolis finished with a 44–16 record, in second place in the Western Division, one game behind the Royals.

During the season, the Lakers continued their series against the Harlem Globetrotters. They were a handicapped team in their game at the Chicago Stadium February 28, as both Jim Pollard and Swede Carlson were nursing injuries and missed the game.

23

Even so, the Lakers held a 24–18 halftime lead, but the Trotters roared back in the second half, behind Goose Tatum, Nat "Sweetwater" Clifton, and Marques Haynes, to win 49–45. The Trotters felt comfortable enough in the fourth quarter to perform some of their crowd-pleasing antics, including a dazzling dribbling routine by Haynes.

The Lakers, though, were at full strength for the return engagement March 14 before 10,122 fans, the largest basketball crowd ever at the Minneapolis Auditorium. With Pollard and Carlson back in the lineup, Minneapolis rolled to a 68–53 win. This time it was the Lakers' turn to clown, and Don Forman delighted the crowd with a dribbling act of his own, one that rivalled the show put on by Haynes two weeks earlier.

The post-season playoffs opened March 23, and Minneapolis had little trouble polishing off the Chicago Stags, as Mikan scored seventy-five points in the two-game sweep.

Next, the Lakers would face Rochester in another best-of-three series in the Western Division finals. The Royals had been without center Arnie Risen the year before when the two teams met for the NBL title. But for this round, Arnie was healthy and ready for the Lakers.

In the first game of the series at Rochester, Mikan continued with the hot hand, scoring thirty-two points. Minneapolis built a seventeen-point lead, but the Royals rallied and carried a two-point edge into the final minute of play. Tony Jaros hit a field goal with eighteen seconds left to tie the game, and, with six seconds to go, Arnie Ferrin dropped a free throw and the Lakers pulled out an 80–79 win,

In Game Two at the St. Paul Auditorium, Rochester held a three-point lead after the third period. But the Lakers held the Royals scoreless from the field in the final quarter, and they outscored them 18–3 for a 67–55 win and a berth in the Basketball Association of America Championship Series.

Kundla and Jaros in a debate with the officials

Their opponents in the four-out-of-seven series were the Washington Capitols. The Caps had cooled after having won their first thirteen games of the season, but they still led the Eastern Division with a 38–22 record.

The series opened in Minneapolis. Mikan scored forty-two in the first game, but it took a pair of free throws by Swede Carlson with forty-seven seconds left to break an 84-all tie en route to an 88–84 win.

The Lakers won the next game, as well as Game Three in Washington to take a commanding lead in the series. The Caps fought back though. Bones McKinney had missed the third game to be with his sick wife in Raleigh, North Carolina. But Bones came back to lead Washington to an 83–71 win in the fourth game. Mikan led the Lakers with twenty-seven points, even though he chipped a bone in his right hand in the first quarter.

George showed up for the fifth game with his wrist in a cast, and the Capitols won, 74–65, to pull within one game in the series.

But that was as close as the Caps would come. The Lakers rolled to an easy 77–56 win in Game Six at the St. Paul Auditorium. The defending National Basketball League champions were now the Basketball Association of America champions.

Mikan had scored 1,698 points during the regular season; he added 303 more in ten playoff games to total 2,002 for the year.

The National Basketball League had been left for dead after the raid by the BAA the year before. But the NBL continued to fight, and following the 1948–49 season, the league signed en masse the graduating starters of the University of Kentucky team which had won the NCAA title. With these players they formed a new franchise to be known as the Indianapolis Olympians (Several of the team's stars had been members of the 1948 Olympic team.) The Indianapolis Olympians would also be jointly owned by its players, which included player-coach Cliff Barker, Wallace "Wah Wah" Jones, Ralph Beard, and Alex Groza. Groza was the brother of Lou "The Toe" Groza of the Cleveland Browns, and he would eventually prove himself second only to Mikan in scoring effectiveness.

This coup by the National League helped pave the way for a merger with the Basketball Association of America before the 1949–50 season.

The BAA had lost two of its teams, the Providence Steamrollers and the Indianapolis Jets, but with the merger came seven NBL teams: the Syracuse Nationals, Anderson Packers, Sheboygan Redskins, Indianapolis Olympians, Tri-Cities Blackhawks, Waterloo Hawks, and Denver Nuggets.

There was only one dominant league in the professional basketball world now, and it took a new name – the National Basketball Association. Over the next five years, the NBA would go through a stage of shaking out the weaker franchises until finally only eight remained.

But in 1949–50, the initial season for the new league, there were seventeen teams, which made division alignments cumbersome and the playoff picture complicated. Teams didn't even play the same number of games during the regular season.

While in Washington for the championship series with the Capitols, Mikan gets his cast signed by Minnesota Senator Hubert Humphrey

1948–49 BASKETBALL ASSOCIATION OF AMERICA CHAMPIONS
Don Forman, Herm Schaefer, Don Carlson, Don Smith, Tony Jaros, Johnny Jorgensen, Earl Gardner, Arnie Ferrin,
Jack Dwan, Jim Pollard, George Mikan

Fans had trouble unraveling and following what was happening on the pro scene. Many didn't bother trying, especially since the collegians were putting on what was possibly their most spectacular year ever, a season that was climaxed by the double championship of Nat Holman's City College of New York team. Loaded with sophomores, the CCNY Beavers won both the NIT and NCAA tournaments, an unprecedented feat.

But excitement for the professional game remained high in the Twin Cities. By this time there was no doubt that Minneapolis had the best team in any league, but during the summer of 1949 the Lakers added two players who would insure that the championship quality of the team would continue.

An All-American from the University of Texas, Slater "Dugie" Martin was an outstanding playmaker, outside shooter and defensive specialist. Dugie (a nickname given to him by his grandfather) would often draw the assignment of covering the opposition's leading scorer.

He had played at Jefferson Davis High School in Houston and led his team to state championship in 1942 and 1943. At Texas, he became the school's all-time leading scorer and set a Southwest Conference record with forty-nine points in one game.

After graduating from the Longhorns, Martin had wanted to go to work for Phillips Petroleum and play with Bob Kurland on the Phillips Oilers basketball team, but when he learned he would be required to sit behind a desk eight hours a day, he instead came to Minneapolis and did his work on a hardwood floor.

Six-foot-seven center Vern Mikkelsen had played high school basketball in Askov, Minnesota, a small community between the Twin Cities and Duluth, and was all set to begin classes at the University of Minnesota in the fall of 1945. During the summer, though, Vern had some misgivings about his choice of colleges when Jim McIntyre, the center who had just led Minneapolis Henry to two consecutive state high school championships, announced his decision to play for Dave MacMillan's Gophers.

Jim Pollard: The Kangaroo Kid

For the seventeen-year-old Mikkelsen, the experience of playing in that tournament "showed me what you had to do to compete against the best."

"I certainly didn't dominate anyone," recalled Mikkelsen years later. "I got a basket off Mikan and I apologized."

Four seasons later Mikkelsen had the chance to face Kurland again when the Phillips Oilers AAU team came to the Twin Cities to play Hamline in a pair of games. Phillips won both games, but Mikkelsen outscored Kurland in each game.

It was that performance that convinced the Lakers to use their territorial draft choice (which allowed a team to pick a player from its own area in the first round regardless of which turn it was entitled to) to select Mikkelsen. But Vern had also piqued the interest of the Phillips people. Oilers coach Jesse "Cab" Renick said, "I hope that kid is interested in the oil business."

Like Slater Martin, Mikkelsen was approached by representatives of Phillips Petroleum, who tried to sell Vern on the stability of the oil business as opposed to going into a "fly-by-night" operation like the NBA.

But, like Martin, Mikkelsen said "No thanks" to Phillips and instead cast his fortunes with the Minneapolis Lakers.

Mikkelsen, Martin, and another newcomer, six-one guard Bob Harrison from the University of Michigan, joined veterans Pollard, Carlson, Mikan, Schaefer, and Jaros as the Lakers, in their third year, in their third league, would pursue their third championship.

Early in the season, Billy Hassett, a two-time All-American for Notre Dame, was acquired from Tri-Cities. In December, Harry (Bud) Grant, a standout in baseball, football, and basketball at Minnesota, left the Gophers and became a Laker.

Grant would average 2.6 points per game each of the two years he played for the Lakers. He then switched sports and pursued a career as an end for the Philadelphia Eagles of the National Football League. After two years with the Eagles he jumped to the Canadian Football League and played for the Winnipeg Blue Bombers. Four years later, at the ripe age of twenty-nine, Grant was made head coach of the team. He led the Blue Bombers to four Grey Cup championships. In 1967 Grant returned to Minnesota as coach of the Minnesota Vikings, whom he took to four Super Bowls.

As a result, Mikkelsen was in a receptive mood when Al Holst, a professor at Hamline University in St. Paul, caught up with Vern in a rutabaga field outside of Askov and persuaded him to switch to Hamline. The Pipers' big man, Howie Schultz, had graduated the year before, leaving an open spot in the pivot.

Although Hamline was considered a small college, it played a national schedule against many major teams. During Mikkelsen's years under Joe Hutton at Hamline, the Pipers played in three NAIB tournaments, winning the national championship in 1949.

During Mikkelsen's freshman year, Hamline played in a 1945 Christmas tournament at Chicago Stadium that included the three premier big men in the country at that time: Don Otten of Bowling Green, Bob Kurland of Oklahoma A & M, and George Mikan of DePaul.

Bud Grant

The Lakers opened their season at Philadelphia against the Warriors and Joe Fulks, who held the only scoring record—sixty-three points in a single game—that didn't belong to George Mikan. Fulks outscored Mikan, 20 to 17, in this game, but Jim Pollard topped them both with thirty points as the Lakers triumphed, 81–69. Minneapolis won its first four games, then settled into a season-long struggle for first place in the Central Division with Rochester.

Mikkelsen saw little playing time as an understudy to Mikan for the first third of the season. But on Christmas against Fort Wayne, Kundla acted upon a hunch he hoped would allow the Lakers to receive maximum benefit from both Mikan and Mikkelsen.

Kundla conceived the idea of a "double pivot" offense, putting Mikkelsen at forward. The result was basketball's first "power forward". Mikkelsen's role was to rebound, set screens, and pick up what Mikan and Pollard didn't do.

"My function wasn't really to score; it was mainly to rebound and play defense," said Vern. "My best scoring nights would come when Mikan and Pollard weren't hitting."

The transition from center, which had been Mikkelsen's position throughout high school and college, to forward was not an easy one. "I had to learn to come on the outside and face the basket with the ball. I developed a two-handed overhead set shot to the extent where it at least kept the defense honest."

At that time, the big men in the game (and, at six-foot-seven, Mikkelsen was considered to be in that class) weren't expected to dribble or shoot from the outside; Mikkelsen's main job was to give Mikan some relief in rebounding chores. "He gave me plenty," asserts George.

With Pollard, Mikan, and Mikkelsen, Minneapolis now had the most formidable front line in the NBA. The virtually impenetrable defensive wall the trio could throw up became even more acute at the Minneapolis Auditorium, where the floor was four feet narrower than that of a normal court. The Lakers would lose only one game at home the entire season.

Alex Groza of Indianapolis gave Mikan his only challenger as the league's top point producer, and George captured another scoring title, averaging 27.4 per game.

Eddie Gottlieb tried a new tactic to slow Mikan, ordering his Warriors to foul George before he could shoot. The rules of the day allowed for only one free throw on a non-shooting foul. But Mikan sank nearly eighty per cent of his free shots that year, making the value of such strategy dubious.

In 1949–50 Minneapolis played two more games against the Harlem Globetrotters and handled them easily, winning 76–60 at the Chicago Stadium in February and 69–54 at the St. Paul Auditorium the next month.

The Lakers finished the regular season with a 51–17 record, tied with Rochester for first place in the Central Division, forcing a tie-breaker playoff game in Rochester. The Royals led by six points with

Mikan battles the Globetrotters' Sweetwater Clifton and Babe Pressley in a February 1950 game at Chicago Stadium

HARLEM GLOBETROTTERS				
NO. NAME	FG	FT	PF	PTS. 1ST HALF
20 Johnny Wilson				
24 Bobby Milton				
29 Louis Pressley				
31 Marques Haynes				
37 Reece Tatum				
40 Nat Clifton				
41 Ermer Robinson				
44 Clarence Wilson				
TOTAL				

MINNEAPOLIS LAKERS				
NO. NAME	FG	FT	PF	PTS. 1ST HALF
99 George Mikan				
17 Jim Pollard				
15 Don Carlson				
13 Tony Jaros				
10 Herman Schaefer				
19 Vern Mikkelsen				
16 Bob Harrison				
22 Slater Martin				
12 Gene Stump				
18 Arnie Ferrin				
14 Paul Walther				
TOTAL				

5¢   *Walnut Hill* /   *Candy Time!*   5¢

The program from a 1950 Lakers-Globetrotters game at the St. Paul Auditorium

three minutes to play, but the Lakers battled back and tied the score. With three seconds left, Tony Jaros let fly with a long set shot that dropped through the basket to give Minneapolis a 78–76 win.

The Lakers then won six straight games to sweep past Chicago, Fort Wayne, and Anderson in the preliminary playoff rounds and earn another berth in the championship round, in which they would meet player-coach Al Cervi and the Syracuse Nationals, led by six-seven forward Dolph Schayes. Schayes was an excellent rebounder as well as an outstanding scorer. He could hit from the outside with a two-handed set shot, or he could drive to the basket, and was adept at drawing a foul to set up a three-point play. And when he got to the free-throw line, he rarely missed. Twice during his career, he sank over ninety per cent of his free throws during the season.

The Nationals were just as formidable on their home court as the Lakers were; like Minneapolis, they had lost only one game at home that year. The Lakers were still confident, however. Rochester had been able to make the same boast until the Lakers beat them in the tie-breaker playoff.

Still, the home-court factor would be significant. Because of a jury-rigged schedule that had given Syracuse a Western Division schedule to play against much easier opposition during the regular season, the Nationals had posted a 51–13 record, the only team with a better winning percentage than Minneapolis. As a result, the Nats were awarded the extra home game in the best-of-seven series, meaning that the Lakers would have to win at least one game in Syracuse's State Fair Coliseum if they were to retain their world title.

In the first game of the series at Syracuse, Mikan scored thirty-seven, but the Lakers were behind, 66–64, with barely over a minute to play. Bud Grant recalls that a play was set up that called for a double pick with Pollard to take the shot. The play produced the desired result, even though it didn't follow its original design. "We swung it around, double picked, the ball went to Pollard and he turned around and threw it to me," said Grant. "I was the most surprised guy in the place, but I took a long shot and it went in to tie the game."

The Nationals came back downcourt and got the ball to Cervi, who drove, shot, and missed. The rebound ended up in the hands of Grant, who passed across the midcourt line to Harrison as the final seconds ticked away. From forty feet out, Bobby unleashed a set shot that dropped as the buzzer sounded. The Lakers had captured the game on the road they needed, 68–66.

Syracuse won the next night to even the series, which would now shift to the Twin Cities.

With the Sportman's Show now occupying the Minneapolis Auditorium, the Lakers were in need of another court. The Armory was also occupied, so they looked across the river at Williams Arena, home of the Minnesota Gophers basketball team. But Minnesota athletic director Frank McCormick, nervous about possible competition for attendance from the Lakers, got his counterparts in the conference to pass a rule prohibiting professional teams from playing in Big Ten facilities. Finally, the Lakers ended up in the St. Paul Auditorium for Games Three and Four.

With over 10,000 fans cramming the Auditorium, the Lakers easily won both games and took a three-game-to-one lead in the series.

Back in Syracuse, the Nationals grabbed Game Five. But by this time, the Minneapolis Auditorium was once again available, and the Lakers would feel right at home in the sixth game.

It turned into one of the wildest affairs ever seen in the playoffs up to that point, but still it was a game that epitomized the style of play prevalent at that time.

Police had to break up a fistfight between Pollard and Paul Seymour; Billy Gabor found himself in two fights, one with Slater Martin and the another with Swede Carlson; player-coach Al Cervi was ejected from the game in the third period; and four Lakers fouled out in the final quarter.

In between all that, Mikan connected for forty points, and Pollard, despite being closely guarded by Seymour, scored sixteen and dished out ten assists. The Lakers rolled to an easy 110–75 victory and their third consecutive championship.

The supremacy of the Lakers was unquestionable. And twenty-six-year-old George Mikan, studying law in the off-season, was carrying pro basketball to new levels of prestige.

1949–50 NATIONAL BASKETBALL ASSOCIATION CHAMPIONS
Slater Martin, Billy Hassett, Don Carlson, Herm Schaefer, Bob Harrison, Tony Jaros, Bud Grant, Arnie Ferrin, Jim Pollard,
Vern Mikkelsen, George Mikan

The Minneapolis Auditorium, shown here during the 1941 state high-school tournament, was the Lakers' first home

Dethroned

Following the first National Basketball Association season, teams in three of the circuit's smaller cities, Sheboygan, Waterloo, and Anderson, withdrew. Denver, because of its distance to other cities in the league, also dropped out. (The Nuggets had lost their first fifteen games of the year and finished the season with an 11–51 record.) Surprisingly, Tri-Cities (which was anchored in Moline, Illinois, but represented Moline and Rock Island, Illinois and Davenport, Iowa) survived; and just as surprisingly, the St. Louis Bombers and Chicago Stags went belly-up.

The demise of the Stags and Bombers resulted in the redistribution of some of the league's stars. High-scoring Max Zaslofsky of the Stags ended up with the Knicks. The league's doormat, the Boston Celtics, picked up center Easy Ed Macauley from St. Louis and Bob Cousy, a guard fresh out of Holy Cross, from Chicago. The Celts had passed on Cousy during the college draft, but now had him back for new coach Red Auerbach.

During the season, the Washington Capitols also folded, leaving the NBA with only ten teams.

Sheboygan, Waterloo, Denver, and Anderson joined a new league, the National Professional Basketball League, a circuit that included the St. Paul Lights, coached by former Hamline University standout Howie Schultz. Like the earlier professional St. Paul team, this one was short-lived. The Lights folded fewer than two months into the season.

For the 1950–51 campaign, the Lakers would be without two familiar faces who had been a part of all three championship teams. Herm Schaefer retired as a player to become a Laker assistant coach and scout; Don "Swede" Carlson also retired and would go on to become the head basketball coach and athletic director at Columbia Heights High School, serving at that suburban Minneapolis school until 1985.

The Lakers were again virtually unbeatable on their home courts. It had been nearly a year since they had lost at home as they prepared for a game against the Fort Wayne Zollner Pistons at the Minneapolis Auditorium November 22, 1950. As it turned out, though, Piston coach Murray Mendenhall had prepared even better.

The tempo of the game became apparent very early. Fort Wayne controlled the opening tip, and Mikan, flanked by Pollard and Mikkelsen, lumbered into defensive position. But as the trio turned around, they saw Piston center Larry Foust standing at midcourt with the ball on his hip. And that's where Foust — and the ball — stayed.

Foust was under strict orders from Mendenhall to do nothing until the Lakers came out to play man-to-man. The standoff was interrupted by an occasional pass, and there was even a brief flurry of action — enough to give Fort Wayne an 8–7 lead at the end of the first quarter.

The stall continued into the next period. Fort Wayne stuck to its game plan, holding the ball and inviting the Lakers to come out and get it, and they ignored the booing and stomping of feet of the 7,021 fans.

Every so often, a bored Slater Martin would try to force a turnover. When he was successful in doing so, the Lakers would hustle downcourt, and after three passes (the last one usually to Mikan), would put up a shot.

But the stall was having its desired effect for the Pistons, as it seemed to unnerve Minneapolis, even on the few occasions when they had possession. Martin missed a fast-break layup in the first period, and Bob Harrison missed another in the second.

A free throw by Mikan with 1:55 left in the half gave Minneapolis an 11–10 lead. After the Pistons re-tied the game, George pushed in another basket with a half minute to go, and the Lakers carried a 13–11 edge into the locker room.

The Lakers held the lead throughout the second half, and even though they were trailing, Fort Wayne continued its tactics. The Lakers, as long as they were in front, were in no hurry to press.

Minneapolis had scored only one point in the fourth quarter, that on a free throw by Pollard, but they still held an 18–17 lead as Fort Wayne inbounded the ball with nine seconds left in the game. With six seconds on the clock Curly Armstrong fed the ball to the breaking Foust, who tried to put one over Mikan's outstretched arms. Mikan, recalls Vern Mikkelsen, got a piece of the ball, but it still dropped through the hoop to give the Pistons a 19–18 lead.

Minneapolis roared back down the floor, but Martin's shot hit off the rim as the final horn went off, ending the lowest-scoring game in the history of the NBA.

Mikan was the game high with fifteen points, and he produced the Laker's only four field goals of the evening.

Comments overheard from the fans leaving the Auditorium included, "It was the best passing clinic I've ever seen. I'm sorry I missed the one on shooting." The spectators weren't the only ones fuming. John Kundla commented, "If that's basketball, I don't want any part of it."

Sportswriter Charlie Johnson called the exhibition a "sports tragedy." But *Minneapolis Tribune* columnist Dick Cullum defended the stall as Fort Wayne's best chance to win: "Therefore, it cannot be criticized for using it. It is a low conception of sports to say that a team's first duty is to give you a lot of senseless action instead of earnest competition."

Cullum also saw the game as a remarkable study in basketball tactics that "in a way, may have been the best basketball game played by the pros in Minneapolis."

League president Maurice Podoloff didn't see it that way, and he immediately summoned the coaches as well as the game officials, Stan Stutz and Jocko Collins, to a meeting. Said Podoloff, "I don't want anything like that to happen again."

Several rule changes were discussed at the meeting, although none were implemented. The problem of stalling would eventually be solved by a shot clock, which would limit the amount of time a team

1950–51 LAKERS
Slater Martin, Joe Hutton, Kevin O'Shea, Tony Jaros, Bob Harrison, Bud Grant, Arnie Ferrin, Jim Pollard,
Vern Mikkelsen, George Mikan

34

could keep possession of the ball without taking a shot. This option, however, was not discussed at the meeting, and it would be nearly four years before the shot clock would be introduced.

The season resumed without a duplication of the Pistons' strategy. On December 15 Pollard fractured his cheekbone and missed fourteen games. Mikan and Mikkelsen carried the load during his absence and stayed within striking distance of first place. Upon Pollard's return, the Lakers passed Rochester to retake the top spot in the Western Division.

They held the lead even though a month later Mikkelsen sprained his ankle and sat out four games (the only games he would ever miss in his ten-year career.)

Minneapolis ended the regular season with the best record in the NBA and finished three games in front of the Royals in the Western Division. The public looked upon the upcoming 1951 playoffs in a new light. For years, the pros had been playing second fiddle to the collegians. But in January 1951, a scandal that would rock the entire basketball world began to unfold. A month later it was revealed that there had been widespread fixing and point-shaving of college games at Madison Square Garden.

Virtually the entire CCNY team, which had won the NCAA and NIT tournaments the year before, was implicated, as were other teams, such as Long Island University and New York University, who used the Garden as their home court.

At first it was thought that the scandals were confined to New York. By the time the investigation was complete, however, there was evidence against thirty-three players at six colleges. Adolph Rupp, the head coach at Kentucky, had bragged, "Gamblers couldn't reach my team with a ten-foot pole."

But Alex Groza and Ralph Beard were found to have taken part in the rigging of games while at Kentucky, and both were drummed out of the NBA before the start of the 1951–52 season. The Indianapolis Olympians, without Groza and Beard, were finished as a gate attraction, although the team itself survived for two more years.

Many more potential pros were cut off because of their involvement. Among them was Bill Spivey, a seven-footer who had succeeded Groza as the big man at Kentucky and who had just led his Wildcats to a victory over Kansas State in the NCAA title game at Williams Arena in Minneapolis.

But college basketball's misfortune proved to be a turning point for the pros. The NBA emerged relatively clean from the scandals and its image was enhanced, although it eventually was revealed that NBA referee Sol Levy had received $3,000 in bribes to affect the outcome of games in 1950.

The Lakers had foiled one of Levy's attempts in the second game of the 1950 season against Washington. Levy had been paid to arrange for a Minneapolis loss by fouling out Mikan. But by the time Levy had called the sixth foul and chased Mikan from the game, George had scored twenty-seven points and the Lakers held on for a 91–85 win.

Other significant events of the 1950–51 season included integration of the NBA when the Boston Celtics selected Chuck Cooper of Duquesne in the second round of the 1950 college draft. Seven rounds later, the Washington Capitols drafted another black, Earl Lloyd of West Virginia State. Over the summer Sweetwater Clifton left the Harlem Globetrotters and joined the New York Knicks, and there were three black players in the league when the 1950–51 season opened.

The NBA's first All-Star game, instigated by Celtic owner Walter Brown, was played at Boston Garden in January 1951. Mikkelsen, Mikan, and Pollard represented the Lakers as players, and John Kundla coached the West squad, which lost to Joe Lapchick's East team, 111–94.

George Mikan beat out Groza and Boston's Easy Ed Macauley to win another scoring title with 1,932 points, averaging 28.4 per game in 1950–51. But in the second-to-last regular-season game, Mikan broke a bone in his ankle and was hobbled as the Lakers prepared for the playoffs.

Minneapolis got by Indianapolis, two games to one, in the opening round. Even with a broken ankle, Mikan scored forty-one in the series opener, but in the second game, a 108–88 loss at Indianapolis, he was held to a career-low two points as he played only fifteen minutes in the game.

The Lakers beat Rochester by three points in the opening game of the best-of-five semi-final series at the Minneapolis Armory, but they dropped the second game, 77–66. The Royals won the next two games at Rochester to take the series and dethrone the Lakers.

Rochester would go on to defeat the New York Knicks in seven games to capture their first, and only, National Basketball Association championship.

Mikan fights for a rebound against the Knicks in Madison Square Garden

Interlude:
The Way It Was

Phi Slamma Jamma, Shake 'n Bake, Showtime, In Your Face. These were hardly the terms that were used to describe basketball in its formative years, in the days before the moves one could make with the ball were viewed as an art form—a type of self-expression. Street cars, not limousines, were the common mode of transportation to the games for the fans.

Slam-dunk contests were unheard of. Few players, in fact, could stuff the ball, and it was rarely done by those who could. One of those, Jim Pollard, explained, "It (the dunk) was thought of as a hot-dog trick." Added Slater Martin, "Back when we played, when a guy got a dunk, the next thing you did was to try to either knock him down or hurt him."

In the very early years of the sport, according to historian Zander Hollander, "games resembled tribal warfare. Walls and pillars in the small gyms would form part of the boundaries, and tactics called for balls and opponents to be bounced off the woodwork."

Basketball had become more civilized by the time Minneapolis got its first professional franchise, but the game of the forties and early fifties could still be distinguished by its roughness. Basketball continues to entail much bruising body contact (and as long as it has large people moving about in a confined area, it always will), but it has had a steady decline in fury compared to what it once was.

The area under the boards was a no-man's land in the early years, and it was virtually impossible to see a foul called as teams fought for a rebound.

The owners were partially responsible for the rough play; they were afraid that if the officials called too tight a game, it would slow up the game. Thus, it made sense for the players to play a physical game.

But the rules themselves also encouraged rough play and fouling. There initially was no limit on team fouls per quarter, and a nonshooting foul garnered only one free throw. It was good strategy to give a player a chance for one free throw, while taking away his opportunity for a field goal. And the foul would often be delivered in such a manner as to leave the shooter a mite discombobulated as he stepped to the line.

With no restrictions on how often the ball had to be shot, a team with a lead had no incentive to increase its margin. Late in the game, when the excitement should have been reaching its peak, the game often deteriorated into a contest of foul trading and the team with the lead would stall.

The Lakers had once been victimized by the slow-down strategy—in their 19–18 loss to Fort Wayne. Only two weeks after that another example occurred as Rochester and Indianapolis played a five-overtime game. The score was 73–73 at the end of regulation play. After five more periods totalling twenty-five minutes, the final score was 75–73 in favor of Indianapolis.

In each extra period the team that controlled the jump held the ball for one shot at the buzzer. One might consider a five-overtime game to be rather exciting; in this one, however, Rochester fans exited en masse while the game was still going on.

There were other games that epitomized both the rough and the tedious style of play of that period.

A playoff game in 1954 between the Celtics and Knicks featured, according to Leonard Koppett in his book, *Championship NBA*, "the sort of distasteful foul-filled, squabbling-and-scrambling, referee-baiting exhibition that was becoming more common." The game, unfortunately for the league, was shown to a national television audience, who didn't even get to see the end of it. Boston won, 79–78, but the game, which lasted three hours, was abandoned by the network before it was finished.

One year before that the Celtics were involved in a playoff game with Syracuse, this one a four-overtime marathon in which 107 fouls were called. There were 130 free-throws shot in the game. Bob Cousy set a new playoff record with fifty points—thirty of them from the free-throw line.

The Nationals' Dolph Schayes had been ejected in the second quarter after a fistfight with Boston's Bob Brannum. (Brannum was also thrown out, but Syracuse considered this hardly an even exchange.)

After Schayes's exit, the Nats had nine players left. Seven of those finished the game with six fouls, which meant that the last three men disqualified were allowed to play, but were charged with a technical foul for each additional personal foul they committed.

Fortunately for the game, this exhibition described by Leonard Koppett as "a lingering death" was not televised and was witnessed only by those present at Boston Garden that afternoon.

The NBA Board of Governors would respond to the problems, however, and in the next few years they would take action to eliminate the stalling and cut down on the fouling and rough play.

The early game featured few men as tall as George Mikan—there weren't that many in the general population to begin with. Centers scored most of their points hooking and wheeling from within the pivot. Guards used a two-handed set shot (some of the more daring used only one hand, but still shot from a set position. The new breed of jump shooters—Jim Pollard, Joe Fulks—operated mainly from the corner.)

With no shot clock in effect, teams could take as much time as they needed, and would get their shots by slowly working the ball to their shooters or inside to their big man.

The result was a tedious style of play which, many said, was characterized by the Minneapolis Lakers. It was said that the Laker attack was as imaginative as a knee in the groin: Mikan, Mikkelsen, or Pollard grabbing a rebound, tossing the ball to Slater Martin who would leisurely dribble into the forecourt as they waited for Mikan to move into the pivot. "Wait for Mikan," said some, had become the Lakers' battle cry.

But John Kundla says the Lakers, contrary to what most people remember, were a team that did a lot of fast-breaking, particularly since, with their Big Three, they could count on getting the defensive rebound. "If we couldn't get the fast break," said John,

"then we'd slow it down and work it into Mikan."

Kundla and one of his former players, Swede Carlson, agree on the fundamental difference between their style of play and the way the game is played now. "The game today is strictly one-on-one," both have said. Kundla adds, "Our half-court offense was really feared. It didn't matter what kind of defense the other team played. If they'd press, Mikan would come out high and it would open up the middle. Back then, you couldn't freelance like they do today. You had to have the plays."

Carlson described a typical Laker play: "I would cut first and (Herm) Schaefer would cut right off my tail. We'd have a forward going across the middle and the guard coming around the outside—things like that—more of a set offense than there is today."

Carlson also recalled another feature of the early game—the absence of a rule prohibiting defensive goaltending. Carlson once played against seven-foot giant Bob Kurland, who would station himself in front of the basket and swat away shots. Says Swede, "You'd come in and fake and fake and fake, try to get him to move, then shoot quickly."

The game was arbitrated by part-time referees. At that time, officiating was not a sole means of income. Even full-time trainers were a luxury whose time had not yet arrived. The Lakers did get trainers in their final years in Minneapolis—Bob Polk, Lloyd (Snapper) Stein, and Glenn Gostick. Before that, "I used to do all the taping," says Kundla. "If there was a serious injury, we'd have to call for a doctor in the house."

Teams travelled with none of the entourage that accompanies a team today and takes care of all their needs. "The first thing we would do when we got to a hotel," said Vern Mikkelsen, "was take out our uniforms and gear and hang it over the radiator so it would dry for the next game. You learned to live with that smell."

As for the travel, it often was far more grueling than the game itself. Initially, a cross-country trip meant train travel. Vern Mikkelsen describes an all-too frequent event for the Lakers: returning home from Rochester, New York. "We often played a Saturday night game there and had to get back to Minneapolis for a Sunday night game. The only way we could make it was the New York Central, which came out of New York City at 8:00 at night and would hit Rochester at 10:22. It wasn't scheduled to stop in Rochester, but we had twelve guys who wanted to get on it, so they'd stop for us.

"We'd watch the clock during the game. If it went into overtime it was a horrible deal. More times than not, we'd end up getting done about 10:12. We wouldn't take a shower, wouldn't even change clothes, you would just put an overcoat over your uniform and grab your clothes, get in the cabs, get to the train, flag it down and get on. We'd spend all night on that train, then catch the 8 a.m. train out of Chicago and get back to Minneapolis at 3:30 or 4:00 in the afternoon and have a few hours before the game that night.

"We spent more time on trains than we did at home. We knew every schedule, every porter, every dining car waiter . . . "

Mikkelsen went on to relate one of the other travails of travel: "Usually we'd get these roomettes on the train, but if you're six-seven, you'd feel like you were in a coffin. There was no way you could stretch out. And if you had claustrophobia, you were in trouble.

"One time someone had screwed up the advance reservations and we couldn't get the roomettes. Instead we had the old-fashioned sleeping cars—the Pullman cars with the curtains and double bunks. All that was left by the time we got on was the upper bunks, and here we had all this stinkin' gear. We hadn't showered, our uniforms were wringing wet, and we hung all that stuff around. They had steam heat at that time, and at about four in the morning, those poor people down below woke up to that odor of our dirty uniforms."

Mikkelsen added that they would look forward to a foul up on the trains, so that they would have to be flown. But even flying at that time was not a sure means of comfort.

Bud Grant remembered a plane trip in which they came across a storm over the Great Lakes: "The plane wasn't pressurized, so we couldn't fly over the storm. To get around it would have taken forever, so they finally decided to fly straight through it. We got knocked and bounced around all over the place. I looked out the window and saw the wing pointing way up in the air. The next time I looked out I almost thought the wing had fallen off, it was pointing so far down."

In the later fifties, the Lakers purchased a DC-3 charter plane (a rebuilt World War II C-47 cargo plane that had flown the Hump during the war, Mikkelsen claimed). But even in this plane a trip from Boston to Minneapolis could take over twelve hours.

"With the prevailing winds being headwinds—west to east—we had to stop four times for gas," said Mikkelsen. "At four in the morning we'd be somewhere in the upper peninsula of Michigan, trying to find someone to bring a gas truck out to refuel." (This same DC-3 would be involved in a harrowing journey with the Lakers in 1960.)

Fred Zollner of the Fort Wayne Pistons was one of the first owners to purchase a plane for his team. And once in the mid-fifties, Zollner offered his DC-3 to the Lakers. It was an offer accepted by all but one.

The Lakers had left Minneapolis one morning for a game that night in Fort Wayne. The temperature was fifteen below zero, the train left Minneapolis late, experienced other problems because of the cold weather, and it was running well behind schedule as it pulled into Milwaukee.

Zollner had been made aware of the train's tardiness and sent his plane to Milwaukee to pick up the Lakers. John Kundla, however, had gone to the dining car and didn't receive the message to get off the train.

"The rest of us got off and stood on the platform as the train pulled out," recalled Mikkelsen. "I still remember the expression on John's face as he looked out the window and saw us. We all waved at him as he wondered what was going on."

Kundla tried to get off the train, but couldn't, and the Lakers were without him as they took the floor in Fort Wayne. Pollard took over as acting coach and got the game started. Near the end of the first half a huge roar went up as the fans spotted Kundla, still in his storm coat, trying to make his way to the Laker bench without being seen.

"I took quite a razzing from the guys for that," said John, "especially since we were ahead by eight when I arrived and we ended up losing by five."

The arena that today houses the Lakers is called the Fabulous Forum. But there was nothing fabulous about the playing venues of the earlier era.

The arena in Baltimore was a converted trolley car barn, and the Pittsburgh Ironmen played on a floor that had huge gaps between the boards, recalled Swede Carlson, who played there while a member of the Chicago Stags. "When you cut, you could feel the edge of the board dig into your foot," said Swede.

In Fort Wayne, the Pistons played in the gymnasium of the North Side High School. Like the gyms of most Indiana high schools of that period, this one had a sunken floor surrounded by concrete walls

Fort Wayne's North Side High Gym was known as "The Snake Pit"

about six feet high. There was little room between the boundary lines and the walls. The bleachers started at the top of the wall and the fans sat almost on top of the players. "Like throwing Daniel to the lions," said Mikkelsen of the arena known by most players as 'The Snake Pit.'

Syracuse's State Fair Coliseum was a musty, dimly-lit arena with very poor ventilation. George Mikan once made the mistake of letting on that the smoke in the building bothered him. "The next time in there," said Mikkelsen, "it seemed like everyone in the place was smoking a cigar. By the third quarter, there were layers of smoke hanging over the floor; you'd have to look between the layers to find your way down court."

The Syracuse Coliseum was also known for its guide-wires, which supported the basket, extending into the crowd. When an opposing team was shooting a free-throw, the fans would yank on the guide-wires, causing the basket to shake.

Playing in Waterloo, the visiting team had to put up with a huge heating unit at one end of the court, which could be turned on to blow hot air on the opposition as they ran up court.

The Rochester Royals played at the Edgerton Park Sports Arena, which had a set of double doors on the wall behind the basket. There was little room beyond the baseline, and a player driving for a layup could go charging through the doors and into four feet of snow. "I did that my first year in the league," said Mikkelsen. "After that you learned to angle off and avoid the doors."

Swede Carlson remembers a similar setup in Midland, Michigan in the arena which housed the Flint Dow Chemical team. "Here they had swinging doors. You could get pushed into them and just swing right around and come running right back in."

But perhaps the oddest arrangement was in St. Louis's Kiel Auditorium, which was a double building. One half was the convention hall with the basketball arena; the other half was a theatre. The stages of the two sides backed up against one another and had a movable wall between them. Out of the locker rooms, a right turn would take a person to the basketball arena. Left was the way to the theatre.

"They'd sometimes have the ballet going on at the same time as a basketball game," said Mikkelsen. "We always had to make sure we went the right direction or we could have ended up right in the middle of Swan Lake."

What would Tchaikovsky have thought?

Three More Titles

The NBA was finally showing some stability as the same ten teams that had finished the 1951 season started and finished the 1951–52 season. There was, however, one shift among the teams as Ben Kerner transferred his Tri-Cities team to a new, 10,000-seat arena in downtown Milwaukee, Wisconsin. It appeared to be a good move, for Kerner and the league, but only a year later the city got its own major-league baseball team, and a baseball-crazed Milwaukee virtually ignored the basketball Hawks. Eventually, Kerner would move his team again in 1955, this time to St. Louis.

Also in 1951–52 the NBA doubled the width of the foul lane (where the three-second rule prevented an offensive player from taking a stationary position) to twelve feet. This move was aimed at the big man in general, and George Mikan in particular, because Mikan did most of his scoring by setting up his pivot play as close to the basket as possible.

The Lakers, obviously, were not enamored with the wider lane. Two years earlier, in response to the league's consideration at that time of widening the lane, General Manager Max Winter stated, "We shall never widen our lane in Minneapolis, and teams may play games here under protest if they care to. If lanes are widened in other arenas, I shall advertise in advance of our games in those towns that George Mikan will not appear on the floor."

Winter never did follow through on his threat, and Mikan adjusted well enough to the new rule, although his scoring average did drop to 23.8 points per game, and he failed to win the scoring title for the first time. Instead, the crown went to a young Philadelphia sharpshooter, Paul Arizin.

The 1951–52 Laker roster included three graduates from Hamline University. Joining Mikkelsen and Joe Hutton, Jr. was Howie Schultz. A native of the area, Schultz had been a baseball and basketball star at St. Paul Central High School, and he chose to continue on in both sports. He starred at center for Hamline from 1940–44 and led the Pipers to the NAIB championship in 1942.

And just as Danny Ainge would do nearly forty years later, Howie combined a college basketball career with one in professional baseball. While still at

Philadelphia marksman Paul Arizin dethroned Mikan as the league scoring champion in 1952

41

Hamline, he played first base for the St. Paul Saints of the American Association and then for the Brooklyn Dodgers.

He concentrated initially on baseball following college. But in 1946 it came to the attention of Anderson Packer coach Murray Mendenhall that the six-foot-six first baseman for the Dodgers could also play basketball. Mendenhall persuaded Schultz to join the Packers after the baseball season ended.

When Schultz reported to spring training with the Dodgers the next year, he lost his starting position at first base to a promising rookie named Jackie Robinson.

By the following year Schultz decided to give up baseball and concentrate solely on basketball. He played for Anderson and Fort Wayne before retiring as an active player and returning to his home state in 1950 to coach the short-lived St. Paul Lights. One year later, he was ready to return as a player and join the Lakers.

From the University of Minnesota, Whitey Skoog

graduated and stepped right into the Laker lineup. With the Gophers, Skoog had introduced the jump shot to the Upper Midwest. High-school players throughout the area copied Skoog's style of shooting. By the time he graduated, he was hailed as the greatest cager in Gopher history.

Skoog, unfortunately, was saddled with knee problems during his rookie year and had to have surgery on his knee, causing him to miss the final three weeks of the regular season as well as the 1952 playoffs. Whitey averaged 6.7 points in thirty-five games.

Also, late in the season, a viral infection forced Mikan to miss his only two games as a Laker. Lew Hitch, a former Kansas State star, filled in at the low post during George's absence.

Earlier in the year, on January 20, Mikan had his best game ever as he scored sixty-one points in a double-overtime win over Rochester. With twenty-two field goals and seventeen free throws, Mikan came within two points of Joe Fulks's NBA record.

Whitey Skoog dribbles past Boston's Bill Sharman

Pollard watches the ball drop through the net for two of his 32 points in a January 1952 game against the Knicks

Kundla again coached the West squad in the All-Star game in Boston, which was won by the East, 108–91. The two men who were battling for the scoring championship, Mikan and Arizin, led their respective teams with twenty-six points each.

Mikan finished the season third in rebounding, but during the season he hauled down thirty-six rebounds in one game, bettering by one the record held by Syracuse's Dolph Schayes.

Even though the Lakers' front line all topped the 1,000-point mark (Mikkelsen and Pollard both reaching that level in the final game of the regular season), Minneapolis finished second in the West with a record of 40–26, one game behind Rochester.

The Lakers easily handled Indianapolis in the opening playoff round, then headed to Rochester for the start of the best-of-five semi-final series against the Royals.

Rochester, attempting to defend its NBA title, won the series opener by ten, despite a forty-seven-point performance by Mikan. The Lakers won Game Two in overtime and had the road victory they needed.

Back in Minneapolis, the Lakers won the third game, but were tied in the closing seconds of Game Four. If they lost, they would have to go back to Rochester for the decisive fifth game. Instead, Pollard stuffed in a missed shot by Mikan with two seconds left to give Minneapolis an 82–80 win and another berth in the championship finals.

The New York Knicks, with Max Zaslofsky, Sweetwater Clifton, Vince Boryla, Harry (The Horse) Gallatin, the McGuire brothers, Al and Tricky Dick, Connie Simmons, and Ernie Vandeweghe, would be the Lakers opponents. New York, under coach Joe Lapchick, was making its second consecutive trip to the finals.

The series opened at the St. Paul Auditorium, and it was Jim Pollard with the hot hand, scoring thirty-four points. Of more significance, however, was a basket by New York's Al McGuire that wasn't counted.

Late in the first period, McGuire drove in, got off a shot, and drew a foul. But what neither official, Stan Stutz or Sid Borgia, saw was that the shot McGuire took went in—even though 10,000 other people in the arena did see it drop.

The Knicks raved, Joe Lapchick protested the game, but the basket remained uncounted. McGuire made one of the two free throws, so the failure of the officials to see his field goal cost the Knicks at least one, and possibly two points.

Those points turned out to be meaningful as the game was tied, 71–71, at the end of regulation play, and the Lakers won the game in overtime, 83–79. The series went the limit, with the Lakers winning the seventh game, 82–65, to capture their fourth championship in five years.

1951–52 NATIONAL BASKETBALL ASSOCIATION CHAMPIONS
Joe Hutton, Bob Harrison, Howie Schultz, Vern Mikkelsen, George Mikan, Lew Hitch, Jim Pollard, John Pilch,
Whitey Skoog, Slater Martin

Pep Saul watches from the floor as Mikan scores in a 1953 playoff game against Fort Wayne

The Lakers opened the 1952–53 season with virtually the same personnel they had the year before. Jim Holstein, a six-three guard from Cincinnati, was the only newcomer.

The team seemed better balanced, however, and they became less dependent on Mikan to do all of the scoring. George's average "dropped" to 20.6 points per game, while Mikkelsen and Pollard averaged 15.0 and 13.0 respectively. Slater Martin took advantage of the collapsing defenses around the Big Three and averaged 10.6 points. In fact, at times Kundla had Mikan and Martin reverse their normal roles. Against certain teams Mikan turned passer and fed Martin breaking toward the basket.

In the All-Star game at Fort Wayne in January, Kundla guided the West to its first win, 79–75, as Mikan scored twenty-two points, pulled down sixteen rebounds, and was voted the game's Most Valuable Player.

The race in the NBA Western Division came down to a contest between Minneapolis and Rochester. The Lakers finished with a 48–22 record, four games ahead of the Royals, the largest margin between those two teams in their four years in the league.

The Knicks won the Eastern Division with a 47–23 mark, one game ahead of Syracuse and Boston, who finished in a two-way tie for second.

The Lakers cruised by Indianapolis and Fort Wayne in the Western Division playoffs. During the Fort Wayne series, they were bolstered by the addition of Dick Schnittker.

Schnittker became property of Minneapolis after the Washington Capitols disbanded two years earlier. But before he could play with the Lakers, Dick wound up in the Army. A six-foot-five forward, Schnittker had been an All-American at Ohio State.

The New York Knicks again emerged victorious in the Eastern Division playoffs. For the third straight

45

year, they would attempt to win the championship; for the second straight year, it would be against the Lakers.

The only major change in the Knick lineup from the year before was that Max Zaslofsky had been traded to Fort Wayne, and Carl Braun was now back from the Army.

Because they had the better record, the Lakers would have the extra home game in the event that the series went the limit. The agenda was for the first two games to be played in Minneapolis, the next three in New York, and the final two (if necessary) back in Minneapolis.

To win the series, the Knicks would have to win at least one game in Minneapolis. They got that win in the first game, 96–88, and nearly took the second game as well, but the Lakers held on to salvage a 73–71 win and a split of the first two games.

It was a jubilant group of Knicks that headed east for the next three games at the 69th Regiment Armory in New York. (In the spring, the circus took over Madison Square Garden, and the Knicks were relegated to the 5,000-seat Armory.)

Vince Boryla, as well as several other Knicks, boldly predicted that the series would end in New York and there would be no need for a return trip to Minneapolis. As it turned out, he was right, but not in the way he had hoped.

In the third game Skoog and Harrison handcuffed Ernie Vandeweghe, while Slater Martin stuck to Tricky Dick McGuire and held the Knick playmaker to two points. Meanwhile, Mikan hit for twenty points, Pollard added nineteen and the Lakers went one up in the series with a 90–75 win.

Game Four came down to the wire. Mikan fouled out with under two minutes left and the score tied.

The Lakers celebrate after winning the 1953 NBA championship at the 69th Regiment Armory in New York

1952–53 NATIONAL BASKETBALL ASSOCIATION CHAMPIONS
Coach John Kundla, Slater Martin, Pep Saul, Jim Holstein, Vern Mikkelsen, Lew Hitch, George Mikan, Jim Pollard, Bob Harrison, Whitey Skoog, Asst. Coach Dave MacMillan

But Skoog untied the score, driving and slanting through a wall of Knicks to drop a two-pointer. A few seconds later Whitey grabbed the rebound on Holstein's missed free throw, put in another field goal, and the Lakers held on to win, 71–69.

There would be no trip back to Minneapolis for the Knicks. The Lakers won the fifth game, making it three straight on the Knicks home court, and following a festive party at the Copacabana, they came home with their fifth championship in six years.

"This title is the sweetest of any of the five we have won as Lakers," said Mikan, who added that he planned to play "at least five more years."

Whitey Skoog, who had played only fourteen minutes per game during the regular season, came alive in the playoffs. After the championship series, Joe Lapchick pointed at Skoog and said, "There's the fellow who beat us. We had no way of stopping him."

The 1953–54 Laker team included four players who would eventually be inducted into the Basketball Hall of Fame: George Mikan, Jim Pollard, Slater Martin, and newcomer Clyde Lovellette, a six-nine graduate of Kansas who had spent a year in AAU competition and was now being groomed as Mikan's successor.

Under Phog Allen at Kansas, Clyde averaged 28.4 points in his career, a record, and established another national record for total points in a career. Lovellette played on an NCAA championship team with the Jayhawks, and he was also a member of the USA gold-medal winning team in the 1952 Olympics.

With Lovellette to back him up, Mikan's playing time dropped to less than thirty-three minutes per game, and his scoring average dipped to 18.1 points. Neil Johnston of Philadelphia won the scoring title for the second straight year, and Mikan finished fourth behind Johnston, Bob Cousy, and Ed Macauley.

The Laker backcourt had Martin and Skoog, spelled occasionally by Frank "Pep" Saul. Dick Schnittker and Jim Holstein would provide the relief for forwards Mikkelsen and Pollard.

The Indianapolis Olympians, still reeling from the expulsion of Alex Groza and Ralph Beard, folded before the season started, leaving the NBA with nine teams.

During the season the Lakers took part in a game against the Milwaukee Hawks at the Minneapolis Auditorium that was played with experimental rules.

The Lakers arrived home from a road trip on March 7, 1954 to find the baskets at the Auditorium two feet higher than normal. The game was to be played with twelve-foot-high baskets, and it was closely watched by many parties. The colleges were considering raising the height of the baskets (Kansas coach Phog Allen had been campaigning strenuously for such a move for many years) and were scheduled to vote on the matter in the next few weeks. A larger than expected crowd showed up for the game.

Advocates of raising the baskets contended that it would deprive the tall man of some of the advantage resulting from his height. Dick Cullum of the *Minneapolis Tribune* disagreed and wrote before the game, "Seems to me the higher basket will hurt the little fellow more than the tall one."

Cullum proved prophetic; after the game, Mikan commented, "It just makes the big man bigger." Clyde Lovellette added, "It kills tip-ins." Indeed, the fans did miss the underbasket excitement.

The Lakers shot only 28.6 percent from the field

Clyde Lovellette would eventually inherit Mikan's spot in the pivot, but not his number 99. Clyde wore number 34 once the regular season opened

in the game, but still managed to beat the Hawks, 65–63. Even so, the idea of higher baskets did not get rave reviews from the participants.

Mikkelsen: "It was a horrible flop. It didn't help the smaller guy. It helped me, the big, strong rebounder, because it gave me another tenth of a second to get set after a shot."

Kundla: "It was a screwy game. Nobody could hit the darn thing. The guys who couldn't shoot hit the most. And the big guys still got the rebound."

Mikan: "It threw the whole game out of sync and made it tougher on the smaller man. With the timing of the ball coming down from the twelve-foot basket, there were more injuries under the boards."

And, according to Pollard, it took some time for the Lakers to get the higher baskets out of their system: "It screwed us up for a week or so."

In that same game, an attempt was made to address another problem, that of the parades to the free-throw lines that too frequently interrupted the game's action. In the first and third quarters of the game, no foul shots were taken during the regular playing time. Instead, they were held "in escrow" and shot at the end of the period.

Like the higher baskets, this experiment was not repeated.

Kundla again coached the West in the All-Star game. Even though his team was losing, Pollard, with twenty-three points, had been named the game's Most Valuable Player in a vote taken in the final minutes of the game. But Mikan tied the game with two free throws with one second remaining in regulation time. In the extra period, Bob Cousy scored ten points to give the East a 98–93 overtime win. Another ballot was taken, and Cousy, not Pollard, was named the game's MVP.

In 1953–54 the Lakers continued to play more and more games on neutral courts. In past years, games on neutral courts were done as part of a doubleheader in another league city. But as the years passed, NBA teams were to play in just about any city in which they could receive a reasonable guarantee.

By the time the Lakers had left Minneapolis, the list of non-league cities in which they had played regular-season games was a long one: Moorhead, Hibbing, and Rochester, Minnesota; Spencer, Des Moines, and Waterloo, Iowa; Minot and Grand Forks, North Dakota; Huron, South Dakota; La-Crosse, Wisconsin; Grand Rapids, Michigan;

Kansas City and St. Louis, Missouri; Elkhart and Huntington, Indiana; Winnipeg, Manitoba; Johnstown, Hershey, and Bethlehem, Pennsylvania; New Orleans, Baton Rouge, and Shreveport, Louisiana; Albany and Buffalo, New York; New Haven, Connecticut; Louisville, Kentucky; Camden, New Jersey; Providence, Rhode Island; Dallas and Houston, Texas; Raleigh and Charlotte, North Carolina; Greenville, South Carolina; Charleston, West Virginia; College Park, Maryland; Seattle, Washington; Portland, Oregon; and San Francisco and Los Angeles, California.

The Lakers finished the regular season with the NBA's best record at 46–26 and again finished four games in front of Rochester in the Western Division.

For the upcoming playoffs the Lakers removed some tables around the Minneapolis Auditorium floor and were able to widen their court from forty-six to the regulation fifty feet.

Since there were only four teams in the Western Division, only three teams in each division advanced to the playoffs, and the NBA tried a system in which the top three teams engaged in a round-robin series to determine two survivors in each division.

Rivals during the regular season, Rochester's Bobby Wanzer (on floor) and Minneapolis's George Mikan were teammates in the 1954 All-Star Game

Minneapolis and Rochester were the survivors in the Western Division; the Lakers then knocked off the Royals, two games to one, to advance to the championship round against the Syracuse Nationals. It would be a rematch of the 1950 championship series for Al Cervi and Dolph Schayes of the Nats and George Mikan, Jim Pollard, Vern Mikkelsen, and Slater Martin of the Lakers, although it would be played with different supporting casts.

The Nats entered the series crippled as Dolph Schayes, with a broken right wrist, played with a cast on. Schayes played only four minutes in the first game, won by the Lakers, 79–68. The second game, in Minneapolis, was nationally televised and won by Syracuse, 62–60, as the Nationals' Paul Seymour hit on a shot from just beyond the midcourt line in the final seconds.

The deadlocked series moved east. The Lakers won two of the three games played in Syracuse, and came back to the Twin Cities needing only one more win to wrap it up.

But the Nats pulled another upset in Game Six. Jim (Rebel) Neal dropped a shot from twenty-seven feet out in the closing seconds to give Syracuse a 65–63 win.

There were 7,274 fans at the Minneapolis Auditorium for the seventh game, and the Lakers, behind Pollard's twenty-one points, got off to a fast start, then cruised to an 87–80 win.

The Lakers had won their sixth championship in seven years; four in the National Basketball Association, one in the Basketball Association of America, and one in the National Basketball League.

They had met all comers and emerged victorious. No one could deny the dynasty.

Slater Martin uses Jim Holstein's screen to move past the Nationals' Billy Kenville during the fifth game of the 1954 championship series, which was won by the Lakers, 84–73

**1953–54 NATIONAL BASKETBALL ASSOCIATION
CHAMPIONS**
*Slater Martin, Pep Saul, Jim Holstein, Jim Pollard, Clyde
Lovellette, George Mikan, Vern Mikkelsen, Dick Schnittker,
Whitey Skoog, Coach John Kundla*

George Mikan: Mr. Basketball

After Mikan

Following the close of the 1953–54 season, the NBA adopted two changes in the playing rules in an attempt to curb the ever-rising number of fouls.

The first was a limit on the number of fouls a team could commit in any one quarter. If they exceeded the limit, the opposing team would receive a bonus free throw. On a non-shooting foul, a team in the bonus would receive two shots instead of one; on a shooting foul calling for two shots, the shooter would have three chances to make two.

The other rule, more revolutionary, was the idea of Syracuse owner Danny Biasone: a time limit on ball possession without taking a shot at the basket. Set at twenty-four seconds, the time limit made it unnecessary for the trailing team to foul deliberately, thus eliminating the steady procession to the free-throw line in the closing minutes.

The result of these rule changes was a vastly different game, heralded almost unanimously. (Merv Harris, author of *The Fabulous Lakers*, said "No decision the NBA Board of Governors ever made has proven more important in broadening the appeal of pro basketball.")

One-hundred-point games became commonplace. The Boston Celtics averaged 101.4 points per game over the entire season, and the league as a whole averaged 93.1 points (up nearly fourteen points per game over the year before).

Many critics wondered how the faster-paced game brought about by the shot clock would affect the Minneapolis Lakers and, in particular, George Mikan. Mikan, never a racehorse to begin with, was now thirty years old. The Lakers style had been a deliberate one, clearing the boards, then making their way down court slowly, waiting for Mikan to lumber into position.

In fact, an outraged Max Winter is reported to have said, "The twenty-four second clock discriminates against George Mikan. It's like baseball legislating against Babe Ruth."

But the question of how Mikan would react to the clock became moot on September 24, 1954. Just three days prior to the opening of Laker practices, George Mikan announced his retirement. By this time, Mikan had passed the bar in Minnesota and planned to open his own law practice.

"I imagine the whole National Basketball Association is rejoicing," said John Kundla of Mikan's decision.

"George Mikan is the greatest all-around basketball player who ever lived and the greatest gate attraction," said Knicks' coach Joe Lapchick. "He's the Ruth, the Dempsey, the Hagen, the Tilden of basketball."

Teammate Jim Pollard described the frustration felt by opposing teams during Mikan's playing days. "Once he stationed himself under the basket, he was tough to push out. For rival players it must have been like trying to move the Statue of Liberty."

Bud Grant, who has seen and coached many great athletes, still maintains, "George Mikan is the greatest competitor I've ever seen in sports."

Some figures to chew on:

At the time of his retirement, Mikan had 11,764 points, topping the next closest player, Joe Fulks, by more than 3,700 points.

In his eight years as a pro, Mikan played on seven league championship teams (six with the Lakers; one with the Chicago Gears).

Four times he led the league in scoring, and he was named to a post-season All-Star team seven-straight years.

Mikan missed only two games in his years with the Lakers. In the 458 regular-season games George played for Minneapolis, 348 times he was the team's leading scorer.

Four times in his career he scored more than fifty points in a regular-season game with the Lakers; twenty-five times he topped forty.

In 1950 the Associated Press voted Mikan the Greatest Basketball Player of the Half Century.

Following his retirement, Oscar Fraley of the United Press said, "George Mikan is six-foot-ten. He couldn't have been greater if he were ten-foot-six."

And, from Les Harrison, the owner and coach of the often-frustrated Rochester Royals: "We would have been the greatest team, not the Lakers, if not for Mikan."

Eleven days after his retirement, Mikan again surprised the basketball world by returning to the Lakers in a new capacity. Max Winter, wanting to concentrate on securing a professional football team for the area (he would eventually be granted the Minnesota Vikings franchise), announced his resignation and revealed that Mikan had purchased his stock and would succeed him as Vice President and General Manager of the Lakers.

Winter had held the title of General Manager since the formation of the Lakers, but often identified as the man who actually controlled the operations of the Lakers was *Minneapolis Tribune* columnist Sid Hartman.

WHO RAN THE LAKERS?
In reality, it was Minneapolis newspaper columnist Sid Hartman, not Max Winter, not Ben Berger, not Morris Chalfen, who was the architect of the Laker dynasty

Bud Grant was quoted by his biographer, Bill McGrane, as saying, "Sid ran the operation, lock, stock, and barrel. He negotiated contracts, signed players, and ran the club."

"Things were a lot different than they are now," said Hartman. "Every guy at our newspaper had a public-relations job with one of the teams. We wer-

en't doing anything behind their backs. The paper knew exactly what we were doing. Charlie Johnson (Hartman's editor) assigned all of these jobs to us.

"You can't do that anymore—it's considered a conflict of interest now. Back in those days, though, it was allowed because you didn't make much money at the paper; we could add a little to our incomes by working with one of the teams. It was a different world back then."

The Lakers with George Mikan had been a championship club. But even without him on the floor, they were still a very good team. They finished the regular season with a 40–32 record, third best in the entire league and the second best in the Western Division, three games behind the Fort Wayne Pistons.

Mikkelsen, the team's new captain, led the Lakers with 19.4 points per game while Lovellette, now starting at center, averaged 18.7 points and 11.5 rebounds per game.

The Rochester Royals had been caught with an aging squad as the 24-second rule shifted the game into high gear, and the Lakers' longtime rivals finished a distant third in the Western Division. (The Royals and Lakers had been classic rivals; for six straight seasons, starting in 1948–49, they had finished one-two in their division. Three times the Lakers finished first; twice it was the Royals, and once it was a tie, with Minneapolis winning a one-game playoff for the title. During that span, no team besides the Royals or Lakers won the league championship. And before that, in their last season in the NBL when they had been in separate divisions, each had won a divisional title, and they met in the final playoff round for the championship.)

In the playoffs the Lakers finished off Rochester in the opening round and met Fort Wayne in the best-of-five division finals.

Playing at home, the Pistons won the first two games. The second game went into overtime tied at 97. Neither team could find the basket in the extra period, and, between them, they missed seven field goals. It finally took a free throw by Max Zaslofsky to give Fort Wayne a 98–97 win.

In Minneapolis the Lakers took Game Three, 99–91, as Whitey Skoog turned in his second-straight twenty-four point performance. But in Game Four at the Minneapolis Armory, Fort Wayne won, 105–96.

The Pistons moved into the championship round, in which they lost in seven games to the Syracuse Nationals.

1954–55 LAKERS
Front: Jim Pollard, Clyde Lovellette, Vern Mikkelsen, Ed Kalafat, Lew Hitch Back: Asst. Coach Dave MacMillan, Slater Martin, Jim Holstein, Dick Schnittker, Bob Carney, Whitey Skoog, Coach John Kundla

The Minneapolis Lakers had, again, been dethroned.

Early in the 1954–55 season, the league was reduced to eight teams when the Baltimore Bullets disbanded. For the NBA, however, the Bullets would be the last team to ever go out of business.

Before the start of the 1955–56 season, Jim Pollard announced his retirement as a player to take the head coaching job at LaSalle College in Philadelphia. The last of the original Lakers, the Kangaroo Kid had averaged in double figures in scoring during each of his eight years with Minneapolis, and he closed his career with an average of 13.1 points per game. The team's first captain, Pollard, along with Mikan, was the only player to be a member of all six Laker championship teams.

George Mikan had been named Basketball Player of the Half Century by Associated Press, but two years later, another poll was taken among players who had been in the league since its inception. Their pick as the greatest player ever? Jim Pollard.

Pollard's spot in the front court would be filled by Dick Schnittker and ex-Gopher Ed Kalafat.

The Lakers exercised their territorial rights to draft six-foot-three Dick Garmaker, a great shooter who held eight scoring records at the University of Minnesota. Garmaker had played two years for the Gophers after transferring from Hibbing (Minnesota) Junior College. In his first year he set a new individual season scoring record with 475 points. The next year he upped that total to 533 points—a 24.2 average for twenty-two games.

The Lakers also picked up another Gopher, Chuck Mencel, for the backcourt. A four-year starter for

Jim Pollard

coach Ozzie Cowles at Minnesota, Mencel held five Gopher scoring records. He had also been named the Big Ten's Most Valuable Player for the 1954–55 season.

The 1955 Laker roster also featured their first black player, Bob Williams from Florida A & M. Williams played two years for the Lakers, although he was cut from the squad early in each of those seasons; each time he joined a Harlem Globetrotter unit.

The Pollard-less Lakers got off to a terrible start, and on November 11 they suffered their worst loss ever, 119–75 at Boston. They dropped to the cellar and, by early December, rumors were flying that General Manager Mikan would return as a player. George said he had no plans to return to the floor, but a month later, it happened.

On Saturday, January 14, 1956, a season-high crowd of over 7,100 jammed the Armory to see the return of the game's greatest player. Mikan entered the game late in the first period and scored eleven points in the twelve minutes he played as the Lakers beat Fort Wayne, 117–94.

With Mikan back, not only did the Lakers climb in the standings, they began to see a return of the larger crowds to the Auditorium and Armory. (Following Mikan's original retirement in 1954, the Lakers went nearly the first two months of the next season before they drew a crowd of over 2,000). In fact, large crowds turned out throughout the league to see Mikan again.

Minneapolis finished the year with a 33–39 record, their first losing season, but it was still good enough for a second-place tie with the St. Louis Hawks, four games behind first-place Fort Wayne.

Behind Slater Martin's twenty-eight points, the Lakers beat St. Louis in a tie-breaker game for second place, then faced the Hawks in the opening round of the playoffs.

Slater Martin is surrounded by Rochester's Bobby Wanzer and Maurice Stokes

Coach Kundla with his troops at the Minneapolis Armory during the 1955–56 season: Slater Martin, Ed Kalafat, Dick Schnittker, George Mikan, Clyde Lovellette, Dick Garmaker, John Horan, Vern Mikkelsen, Lew Hitch, Whitey Skoog

The Hawks overcame a nineteen-point deficit to win the opener of the best-of-three series, 116–115, but the Lakers won the second game, 133–75. The fifty-eight-point spread was the largest in NBA history, and all ten Lakers scored in double figures in the game.

In the deciding game, the Hawks' Al Ferrari dropped two free throws with fifty-four seconds left to give St. Louis a 116–115 win. The Lakers had outscored the Hawks by fifty-six points in the three games, but had lost the series.

There were new faces in Minneapolis, as well as throughout the NBA, in 1956–57.

The Lakers had determined that Clyde Lovellette could not carry the load in the pivot, so they acquired seven-foot Walter Dukes in a trade with the Knicks. At Seton Hall, Dukes had become the first player to

ever average twenty points and twenty rebounds per game for his entire college career. In exchange for Dukes, the Lakers gave up Slater Martin, a member of four of their championship squads. (Martin was later traded to St. Louis, where he would play on another championship team.)

In the meantime, the Boston Celtics traded a pair of future Hall-of-Famers, Cliff Hagan and Easy Ed Macauley, to St. Louis for the draft rights for a center who would not be available until December, after the completion of the 1956 Olympics in Melbourne, Australia. The player was worth waiting for, however; his name was Bill Russell.

The Rochester Royals had the first pick in the college draft that year. The Royals decided to pass on Russell, though. They already had a center, Maurice Stokes, so they used their number-one pick to draft

Sihugo Green, a muscular guard from Duquesne. The Royals were also scared off by Russell's public statement that he would want a $25,000 salary to play in the NBA. (The Harlem Globetrotters had reportedly offered Russell a similar salary to tour with them.)

The number-two pick in the draft belonged to St. Louis, but Hawks' owner Ben Kerner also wanted no part of Russell. They already had six-nine Bob Pettit at center, Kerner also balked at Russell's price tag, and there was concern over how Russell, a black, would be accepted in St. Louis. The Hawks were the last all-white team in the NBA.

Meanwhile, the Lakers, with the number-three pick, were poised to draft Russell and fill the hole at center that had existed since the retirement of Mikan. But Kerner foiled the plot by trading his draft pick to Red Auerbach, and Russell instead became a Celtic.

How close had the Lakers come to getting Russell? The year before the Lakers and Hawks had tied for the second-worst record in the league, but the Lakers defeated the Hawks in a tie-breaker playoff game. Had they lost that game, they would have drafted ahead of the Hawks and would have been able to select Russell.

Sid Hartman also reports that a trade the Lakers almost made in February 1956 would probably have assured them the opportunity to draft Russell. The Lakers were set to trade Vern Mikkelsen to the Celtics for former University of Kentucky greats Cliff Hagan, Frank Ramsey, and Lou Tsioropoulos, all of whom were in the service at the time and would have not been available until the following season.

Hartman theorizes that, with Mikkelsen gone, the Lakers would have finished last and had the first pick in the draft. But Laker owner Ben Berger was talked out of making the trade, and the dynasty that may have been created had the Lakers obtained Russell, along with Tsioropoulos and future Hall of Famers Hagan and Ramsey, never happened.

Hartman added that, because of this, he decided to end his involvement with the team. "It was at that time that I had to decide whether to stay with the newspaper or go full time with the Lakers. When Berger called off the Mikkelsen deal, I told him, 'I'm done. Get somebody else to run the team.' I finished out the rest of the season and then I was gone."

The Celtics had been the league's weakest team their first four years. They became stronger, but still fell short, in the next six years. The Celtics had never

A 1956 trade involving Vern Mikkelsen that never materialized could have drastically altered the course of history for both the Lakers and the Boston Celtics, as well as the entire National Basketball Association

won a division title, nor had they ever reached the championship round of the playoffs. That was before Russell, who would rewrite the book on how defense was played under the basket.

Boston won the Eastern Division with a 44–28 record. The last place team in the East, the New York Knicks, finished at 36–36, a record better than that of any team in the West. The entire Eastern Division had finished ahead of the Western Division.

In the West, the Lakers finished in a first-place tie with St. Louis and Fort Wayne, all with records of 34–38. In tie-breaker games, the Hawks defeated the Pistons and then the Lakers to earn a first-round bye in the playoffs.

Minneapolis beat the Pistons in the opening round, but they were no match for the Hawks, whose lineup featured four men now in the Hall of Fame: Slater Martin, Ed Macauley, Cliff Hagan, and Bob Pettit. St. Louis swept them in three straight, although the Lakers did push the Hawks into double-overtime in the final game.

The Hawks and Celtics then met in what is regarded as one of the greatest championship rounds ever. The series went the full seven games. Boston prevailed in the finale, 125–123, in double overtime. It was the first NBA championship for the Celtics. The first of many.

Pollard, Mikkelsen, and Mikan. A 1957 reunion of basketball's greatest front line

There was other drama brewing, however, as the 1957 season drew to a close. In late February, the Lakers' two owners, Ben Berger and Morris Chalfen (Berger by this time had purchased Mikan's stock; he now owned two-thirds of the team and Chalfen one-third), received an offer of $150,000 for the team from two St. Louis businessmen, Milton Fischman and Marty Marion (the ex-St. Louis Cardinals' shortstop).

Fischman and Marion had earlier been turned down in attempts to purchase the Syracuse Nationals and then the Rochester Royals. If they were successful in buying the Lakers, they planned on moving the franchise to Kansas City.

Berger was ready to accept the duo's offer, but finally sold only an option to buy, so the sale would go through only if Minneapolis interests could not match the offer by March 13.

George Mikan immediately offered to mortgage his home to make a down payment on the team, but he was turned down by Berger, who said he had agreed to sell only to a group or civic organization.

In the meantime, *Minneapolis Star* sports editor Charlie Johnson initiated a drive to sell $200,000 in stock in a corporation to purchase the Lakers. (Johnson had earlier been involved in a bond-selling drive to raise money for the construction of a new baseball stadium south of the city limits; he had also started a task force to try to lure a major-league team to play in that stadium.)

Within ten days the goal was reached—with twenty-four hours to spare before the deadline. Fifty-thousand dollars was kept for operating capital (it was depleted within a few weeks). The other $150,000 was turned over to Ben Berger, president and majority owner of Minneapolis Basketball, Inc.

It was the end of the line for Berger as owner of the Lakers, although he would remain a visible figure in the city.

Born in Ostrowiec, Poland in 1897, Berger came to America at the age of sixteen. His parents and sisters stayed behind and eventually perished in the ovens of Treblinka during the Holocaust. Berger built a theatre empire and at one time owned as many as nineteen movie houses in Minnesota and neighboring states. He also operated Schiek's Cafe in downtown Minneapolis.

After selling the Lakers, Berger became owner of the Minneapolis Millers of the International Hockey League, was a commissioner on the Minneapolis Park Board, and was a founder and first president of Amicus, an organization that works with prisoners and helps ex-convicts to adjust to life outside of prison. Berger stayed active in civic affairs and philanthropic endeavors until his death at the age of 90 in 1988.

With the departure of Berger and Chalfen, 117 firms and individuals assumed ownership of the Lakers. A fifteen-member board of directors was named, and local attorney, trucking magnate, and political maverick Bob Short was elected president.

The Syracuse Nationals were the only other team in the league to be owned by a group of stockholders. When the future of that franchise had been in jeopardy in 1954, a group of 150 men pooled their money and purchased the team.

The merits of this type of ownership were debatable. Charlie Johnson later wrote in the *Minneapolis Star*, "Everyone who invested money got in his lick on how to run the operation. As a result, one mistake after another was made."

Vern Mikkelsen concurred and said that this was the point at which the franchise began to fall apart: "With over 100 investors, it was not a good deal. We had 100 bosses, and a half-dozen of these guys were constantly telling us what we should do and how we should do it. These were people who had never been closer to a locker room than walking by one when they were in high school."

But, regardless, the franchise was saved. The Lakers would remain in Minneapolis—for the time being.

*Ben Berger, right, turns over the Minneapolis Lakers to new
owner Bob Short*

Mikkelsen scores against the Pistons in the opening game of the 1957 playoffs at the Minneapolis Armory

The New Lakers

The new ownership tried to create broader interest in the team by dropping the name of the city from the title. For the next year, it would not be the "Minneapolis Lakers." Instead the club was to be referred to as the "New Lakers."

The New Lakers did have a new look in 1957–58. For the first time, John Kundla would not be on the bench. Kundla had tired of the stress and, particularly, the travel demands. So when he was given the choice by the new ownership of coaching or becoming general manager, he opted for the latter job. At Kundla's suggestion, the new coach would be George Mikan.

Mikan quickly found out what dealing with the new ownership would be like. "They told me I would have complete control of the team and would be able to pick my own personnel," he said. "Then, in one swoop, they got rid of Walter Dukes, Clyde Lovellette, and Ed Kalafat and got a bunch of little guys."

The National Basketball Association also had a new look. Fort Wayne had moved to Detroit, and Rochester to Cincinnati. Only three years before, half the NBA's teams had been in metropolitan areas of less than a million people; now only Syracuse was in that category.

For the Lakers, Schnittker, Mikkelsen, and Bob (Slick) Leonard were the only holdovers from the year before.

The Lakers' new look on the floor included a flashy star out of the University of West Virginia, Hot Rod Hundley, the most publicized player to graduate that year.

Hundley was exceptional as a scorer and ball handler, and he was the first player selected in the 1957 college draft, taken by Cincinnati. The Royals then traded Hot Rod to the Lakers for Clyde Lovellette, who had worn out his welcome in Minneapolis. Hundley never matched his college exploits in his six years as a pro, but his style made him a crowd favor-

Hot Rod Hundley

ite. As an announcer, following his playing days, Hundley was fond of recalling one of his "greatest performances"—the game in which he and Elgin Baylor combined for seventy-eight points. (Elgin had seventy-one of those points.)

Besides Lovellette, Walter Dukes was also gone. Their place at center was filled by veteran Larry Foust (the man who had scored the winning basket in Fort Wayne's 19–18 win over the Lakers in 1950).

Another fixture in the Laker lineup was also missing. Whitey Skoog, whose career was hindered by knee and back injuries, had played in only twenty-three games the year before and announced his retirement at the age of thirty.

During the season, the Lakers picked up Frank Selvy, a great outside shooter, from the Hawks. Selvy had once scored 100 points in a college game while playing for Furman. On eight other occasions he scored fifty or more, and he finished his collegiate career with a 32.5 points per game average.

When the season opened, the Lakers got off to their worst start ever, losing their first seven games. Coach Mikan seemed less comfortable in a suit and tie than he was in shorts and sneakers, and he often had trouble controlling his energy on the bench.

During a game in November, George jumped straight up and out of his chair in response to an official's call, and he was ejected. Mikan retired to the balcony of the Minneapolis Auditorium and communicated by phone with Kundla, who had come out of the stands to take over as acting coach.

In January, Kundla replaced Mikan on the bench again, but this time it was for keeps. With the teams's record at 9–30, owner Bob Short fired Mikan as coach. George was offered the chance to be General Manager again, but he decided instead to return to his law practice.

As a result, Mikan was not around to see his single-season record of 1,932 points broken. In a game against the Lakers, Detroit's George Yardley scored forty-nine points to surpass Mikan's old total. Yardley would go onto to become the first player to

Dick Garmaker drives past the Pistons' George Yardley. Garmaker is an alumnus of the University of Minnesota and Hibbing (Minn.) High, the same schools that would later produce Boston Celtic star Kevin McHale

top the 2,000-point barrier in the regular season. (A few years later, a fellow named Chamberlain would score over 4,000 points.)

The Lakers improved slightly with Kundla back at the helm, but they still ended the season at 19–53, fourteen games behind the next-worst record in the league. The Lakers were winless in nine games against the Boston Celtics, who produced the best regular-season record in the NBA, although they would be beaten by the St. Louis Hawks in the championship round.

Even though the Lakers had great difficulty in beating anyone else in their league, they had little trouble in defeating the Harlem Globetrotters. It was the first meeting between these teams since 1952; it would also be the final game of what had been a great rivalry through the years. The Globetrotters had won the first two games they played, but the Lakers had won the final six.

When these exhibition contests began in 1948, the Globetrotters were a legitimate challenger for the right to claim themselves as the world's greatest team. But with the integration of the NBA, the Trotters no longer had a monopoly on the best black players. Relying more and more on their comedy routines, the Globetrotters, as they do to this day, remained a great attraction. In fact, for many years, the NBA saw its largest crowds when their game was a part of a doubleheader on the same bill with the Globetrotters.

Suffice it to say, the New Lakers did not see great crowds in 1957–58. Now Bob Short, hailed as the savior a year before, started rumbling about possibly moving the team. "At our present artistic and financial pace," said Short at mid-season, "we couldn't operate here next season."

But the shrewd Short was able to alleviate both the artistic and financial problems by the time the 1958–59 season opened.

If the Lakers couldn't draw at home, Short surmised, he would take the show on the road. The Lakers ended up playing twenty-four games on neutral courts, one-third of their entire schedule and two more games than they would play in the Twin Cities.

Short also stayed solvent and increased revenues by raising the ticket prices, which had ranged from ninety cents to $2.40, to a range of $1.50 to $4.50.

And the Lakers worst record in the NBA would also give them the first choice in the 1958 college draft.

The number-one senior in the country that year was Archie Dees of Indiana. But the man every team wanted was Seattle University's Elgin Baylor, a junior who was eligible for the draft because he had sat out a year after transferring from the College of Idaho.

Baylor had been the nation's leading rebounder in 1957, and had led the Seattle Chieftain's to the NCAA title game, which was won by Kentucky, in 1958. But Baylor had publicly stated that he would not turn professional that year and would return to finish his senior year at Seattle.

With his franchise facing extinction, however, Bob Short decided to gamble. He used his number-one draft choice to pick Baylor, and, after several months of negotiations, signed him to a Laker contract. "If he had turned me down, I would have been out of business," said Short. "The club would have gone bankrupt."

With his exceptional driving ability and his twisting, driving layups in which he often changed direction in mid-air, Baylor caused the terms "body control" and "hang time" to become part of basketball lexicon.

He could and would make the effort to follow his own shot. Even though such statistics are not kept, many have said Baylor holds the record for making baskets after rebounding his own missed shot.

John Kundla called Elgin, "the greatest find since Jim Pollard."

The other new players on the 1958–59 Laker team were forward Alex (Boo) Ellis and six-foot-eight Steve Hamilton, who a few years later would become an ace southpaw in the New York Yankees' bullpen.

The Lakers defeated Cincinnati, 99–79, in their opener. Baylor, in his NBA debut, scored the Lakers' first eight points and was game high with twenty-five points.

Because of their precarious situation the previous two years, the Lakers had been placed under financial probation by the NBA, meaning that if they could not average gate receipts of $6,600 per home game, the league would have the right to take over the franchise for $150,000. But the league never had the opportunity to exercise that privilege.

With the coming of Baylor, the Lakers saw the return of large crowds at the Minneapolis Auditorium, and the probation was lifted in January 1959. The Lakers would average 4,122 paying customers per game for the season, compared to 2,790 the year before.

The Lakers had by far been the worst team in the league the previous season, but in 1958–59 they came back to finish 33–39, good for second place in the West (although still sixteen games behind the division-champion St. Louis Hawks).

The resurgence of the team could be traced to the spectacular play of Baylor. On February 25, Elgin scored fifty-five points in a game, the third highest total ever, behind Mikan's 61 and Joe Fulks's 63. Elgin averaged 24.9 points per game for the season, placing fourth behind Bob Pettit, Jack Twyman, and Paul Arizin. He was named Rookie-of-the-Year and made the NBA post-season All-Star team (Bob Pettit and Alex Groza were the only other players to accomplish this as rookies). Baylor finished third, behind Bill Russell and Pettit, in the voting for Player of the Year.

Baylor missed only two games during the season: one because of illness; the other was for a different reason.

Baylor moves past the Hawks' Bob Pettit

The Lakers played many games that year in neutral cities south of the Mason-Dixon line. There were three blacks on the team—Baylor, Boo Ellis, and Ed Fleming—who were not allowed at hotels that the Lakers normally would have stayed at. Bob Short insisted that the Lakers stay together on the road, and the entire team would find lodging that allowed blacks.

In Charleston, West Virginia, however, Baylor became upset when he was refused service at a restaurant, and as a result, he refused to dress for the Lakers' game that evening against Cincinnati. Without Baylor, the Lakers lost to the Royals, 95–91.

The Charleston American Business Club, who had sponsored the game and had counted on Baylor as a gate attraction, asked league president Maurice Podoloff to discipline Baylor and the Lakers.

Podoloff, however, sided with the Lakers, and Bob Short stood behind Baylor. "That shows there's a guy who believes in principle," said Short of Baylor. "I don't argue with principle."

The two best teams in the NBA that year were easily Boston and St. Louis, and fans anticipated the third-straight meeting between those teams in the championship round.

But the Hawks never made it.

In the Western Division finals, St. Louis won two of the first three games against the Lakers. But Minneapolis took the final three games, and it was the Lakers, not the Hawks, who would meet Boston for the title.

Kundla recalls that he didn't need a "Win One for the Gipper" speech during the series with St. Louis. Instead, Bob Short came into the locker room at half time and promised gifts for the players if they won. "One night it was blazers; the next night it was a new set of tires," said Kundla. "I didn't have to say much after that. The guys would almost knock me down getting out of the locker room and back onto the court."

The prognosis for Minneapolis was not good for the upcoming series with Boston, however. Baylor was slowed by a severe bruise on his left knee. And fans wondered how the Lakers, even with a healthy Baylor, would handle the Celtics.

Boston had won their last eighteen games against the Lakers. And only a month before, the Celtics had defeated the Lakers, 173–139. The 173 points by Boston remains a record for a regulation game, exceeded only by a triple-overtime game in 1983 in which Detroit defeated Denver, 186–184. Bob Cousy also set a record (which has since been equalled and later broken) with twenty-eight assists in the game.

Seven players scored twenty or more points in the game: Tom Heinsohn 43, Bob Cousy 31, Bill Sharman 29, and Frank Ramsey 20 for Boston; Elgin Baylor 28, Vern Mikkelsen 25, and Rod Hundley 21 for Minneapolis.

League president Maurice Podoloff called the score "unbelievable", and although he later denied it, he reportedly was planning an investigation to make sure that the players hadn't been "goofing off" on defense.

The Lakers couldn't break the Celtic hex in the playoffs. Boston swept the championship series in four games, the first time a sweep had ever happened in the final round. This would be the first of eight-straight NBA championships for the Celtics.

Even so, for the Lakers there was cause for great optimism. In three of the games in the series against Boston, the Celtics' margin of victory was five points or fewer.

A team that had won barely twenty-six per cent of its games the year before had come back to make it to the championship round. And a team that had started the season in danger of being taken over by the league because of low attendance, saw several home crowds in excess of 10,000 fans during the playoffs, attendance figures that hadn't been reached since their championship years.

Larry Foust battles for position with Bill Russell during Game Three of the 1959 championship series. Despite Foust's 26 points, the Celtics won the game, 123–120

The Lakers had high hopes for the coming year, but they would open the 1959–60 season with a new leader. The day after the playoff series with Boston ended, Kundla announced his resignation to accept the head coaching job for the Minnesota Gophers, replacing Ozzie Cowles, who was stepping down after eleven seasons at the helm.

Kundla had been with the Lakers from the beginning, and had compiled a 466–319 record in his eleven-and-a-half years as coach. Only Red Auerbach had more professional coaching wins.

Another Laker landmark also stepped down. After ten seasons and 699 games (both Laker records), Vern Mikkelsen decided to get out and devote more time to his family and insurance business. A tremendous rebounder throughout his pro career, Mik also scored 10,063 points and averaged 14.4 per game. He hit a career high forty-three points in a game barely two months before his retirement.

Mikkelsen was one of the game's most durable performers, having played in 642 consecutive games, a record at that time surpassed only by Harry Gallatin of New York and Detroit.

Bob Short did his best to persuade Vern to hang on as a player and also coach the Lakers. Short offered the Great Dane a $25,000 salary and 25% ownership of the team, but Mikkelsen demurred.

Vern still remembers coming to breakfast in 1965 and having his wife show him the headline that Short had sold the Lakers to Jack Kent Cooke for $5 million. "And she knew exactly what 25% of five-million dollars was," lamented Mikkelsen.

John Castellani

To replace Kundla as coach, thirty-two-year-old John Castellani was hired. Castellani had been Elgin Baylor's coach at Seattle University and had been the freshman coach at Notre Dame before that. According to writer and former NBA historian Leonard Koppett, the hiring of Castellani was "simply to keep Elgin happy (in a way that was, really, both an insult and injustice to Baylor). But it made the point as to who was important."

(Another example of Baylor's importance manifested itself in 1959 when Elgin fulfilled his military commitment by going through and Army Re-serve Medical Corps training program in San Antonio, Texas. This took place during the Lakers' preseason practice. Short transferred the team's training camp to San Antonio so that Baylor could take part in it, too.)

Rudy LaRusso of Dartmouth also joined the Lakers in 1959. The six-eight LaRusso was the first Ivy Leaguer to step into the NBA in six years.

For the team's first twelve years, the Minneapolis Auditorium had been the Lakers' primary court for home games, with the Armory, St. Paul Auditorium, and even Norton Fieldhouse on the Hamline campus in St. Paul being used in a pinch.

But in 1959 Bob Short pumped some dollars into the Minneapolis Armory, adding new seats and a new floor, as well as other improvements, and the Lakers had a new home.

Their first game in the renovated Armory was the season opener—a 106–105 loss to Detroit despite fifty-two points by Baylor.

Elgin topped that total three weeks later against Boston, a team that had beaten the Lakers in their last twenty-two meetings. This time, however, Minneapolis prevailed, 136–113, as Baylor scored sixty-four points, breaking by one Joe Fulks's NBA record, which had stood for over ten years.

But the Lakers needed more than Baylor. Bob Short again asked Mikkelsen to return, even if only for home games. But Vern was tied up in his insurance business and was also coaching basketball at Breck High School in Minneapolis.

On January 2, 1960 the Lakers had an 11–25 record, and Castellani resigned as coach. Jim Pollard, back in the Twin Cities after having coached at LaSalle College for three years, was hired to coach the Lakers the rest of the season.

Pollard returned just in time to take part in the most exciting journey in the history of the Lakers.

By this time, train travel was a thing of the past for the Lakers. The year before Bob Short even purchased a DC-3 for the team. (A converted World War II C-47 cargo plane, the DC-3 was the usual commercial plane of this era.)

Early in the morning of January 18, 1960, Short received a call from the Civil Air Patrol informing him that his plane was missing—with his entire basketball team on board.

The Lakers had played an afternoon game the day before against the Hawks, and their plane had left St. Louis in a snowstorm that night. In addition to the

Baylor watches as his jump shot from the corner sails toward the basket. Baylor scored 64 points in this game to set an NBA record

crew and the Lakers, there were six adults and four children, including one of Pollard's, on board.

According to the copilot, Harold Gifford, "We shouldn't have taken off. There was freezing drizzle with only a three-hundred foot cloud ceiling and three-quarters of a mile visibility. It was my decision that we not go." But Gifford was overruled by pilot Vern Ullman, and the DC-3 departed for Minneapolis.

Shortly after takeoff, the lights in the cabin died. "I thought it was one of our guys joking around," said Pollard. "But when I got to the front, I saw the copilot shining a flashlight on the instrument panel, and all the instruments were dead." The electrical system had failed. There were no guidance instruments except a compass, but soon that failed as well. With no power for the radio to let anyone on the ground know what was going on, they couldn't risk returning to St.

Louis, so they headed north in the general vicinity of Minneapolis. Ullman climbed above the storm, picked up the North Star, and flew by magnetic compass.

There was no heat in the plane, and the cockpit windows had to be left open because the defrosters didn't work.

"Except for wondering how we were going to get down, the flight was great," Pollard remembered. "It was smooth, although there was no heat or light. The players took whatever blankets we had and gave them to the kids."

Five hours after takeoff, the DC-3 had drifted off course. Its crew and their Laker cargo were somewhere over western Iowa — very low on fuel. Finally the crew spotted the lights of a small town below and circled it, searching desperately for an airport. They dropped down and began following a blacktop road,

69

hoping it would lead them to an airstrip. The visibility was poor enough because of heavily blowing snow, but the problem became more treacherous because the windshield was frosted over. Gifford finally realized that the road had curved off and they were now very close to a grove of trees. He pulled the control column back and the plane shot upward, narrowly missing the trees.

"We came within a couple of seconds of a crash right there," said Gifford. "We were just about ready to hook a wing tip into those trees; if we had, the plane would have cartwheeled, and we would have all died."

After the near miss, they turned around and followed the road back into town. Ullman wanted to land on the highway, but Gifford opted instead for a nearby cornfield. "I was a farm kid, and I knew there would be no rocks or ditches in the cornfield," he said. Unable to see out the windshield, Ullman stuck his head out the side window and brought the plane down. The aircraft slid for about a hundred yards before coming to a stop. A joyous group of passengers, all safe, jumped out of the plane into knee-deep snow.

People from nearby Carroll, Iowa gathered quickly at the landing site and gave the players rides into town. Pollard was the last of the Lakers to leave. He got into a long car, and discovered that the driver was also the local undertaker and that the vehicle in which he was riding was a hearse. "I had not been scared in the least while we were in the air or when we were landing," said Pollard. "But when I saw that stretcher in the back of the car, I realized how close we had come, and I got the shakes for a few minutes."

In addition to the passengers, the plane also survived the ordeal, and it continued to serve the Lakers.

One week after the close shave, the Lakers traded

The Lakers' plane rests in an Iowa cornfield after a forced landing in January 1960

Dick Garmaker to the Knicks for center Ray Felix. For the first time, the Minneapolis roster would have no Minnesota Gophers. Ten alumni from Minnesota had played for the Lakers through the years: Don Carlson, Tony Jaros, Don Smith, Warren Ajax, Kenny Exel, Bud Grant, Myer (Whitey) Skoog, Ed Kalafat, Chuck Mencel, and Garmaker.

Minneapolis finished in third place with a 25–50 record and upset Detroit in the opening playoff round. Their opponent in the division finals would be St. Louis, who had finished the regular season at 46–29. The Hawks took the first game at home, but the Lakers won the second, 120–113, behind Baylor's forty points. At the Minneapolis Armory, St. Louis won Game Three and led by twelve at the half in the fourth game. The Lakers, though, came back to win, 103–101. Baylor had thirty-nine points, including the game-winning basket with forty-two seconds left. Elgin then stole the ball from Cliff Hagan to preserve the win.

The Lakers shocked the Hawks by winning the fifth game, 117–110 in overtime, as Baylor again scored forty points. But back in the Armory, St. Louis stayed alive with a win in Game Six.

The series, and the right to face the Boston Celtics, would come down to the seventh game in St. Louis. Despite thirty-three points from Baylor, the Lakers' season ended as they fell to the Hawks, 97–86.

There was drama beyond the outcome of the Lakers' games, however, as, once again, it began to look as though the Lakers would not be in Minneapolis much longer.

In late January, Bob Short had said, "If we can't sell 3,000 season tickets in advance for next season, then we'll have to move."

A month later Short said that attendance in the team's final home games would weigh heavily in his ultimate decision on the future of the Lakers.

One of the Lakers' final home games was against the Philadelphia Warriors and their record breaking rookie, Wilt Chamberlain. A season-high crowd of 5,172 turned out, but Short remained unimpressed. Said Bob, "Chamberlain would draw more than this anywhere."

Meanwhile, the NBA had given Bob Short permission to move the Lakers. No specific city was mentioned, but it was no secret that Los Angeles was his first choice. Short had even transferred a couple of home games to Los Angeles to test the interest of West Coast fans. (Those games were played in late

January, shortly after the close call in the Iowa cornfield. The same plane was used for the journey over the Rocky Mountains and to the coast. There were more than a few nervous players on board.)

No official announcement regarding the team's future had been made when the season ended. But, as it was with the Brooklyn Dodger followers fewer than three years before, the Minneapolis fans could sense that this was the end.

"This time the city was ready for the decision," wrote Charlie Johnson in the *Minneapolis Star*. "Many hoped it wouldn't happen, but just as many got so tired of the threats that they lost interest."

And when the Minneapolis Lakers played their final game, March 25, 1960 in St. Louis, the locals paid little attention. Their interest instead was riveted on the final game of the state high school basketball tournament, played that same evening, in which the team from tiny Edgerton completed its Cinderella season with still another upset to capture the state championship.

On April 28, it became official. "When you are in trouble," said Bob Short, "you have the choice of selling, taking bankruptcy, or operating your way out. We are going to do the latter," and the Lakers were Los Angeles bound, where a 14,000-seat arena had recently been constructed adjacent to the Los Angeles Coliseum.

Short wasn't sure if the West Coast would be the answer to his problems, but he felt he had to take the team somewhere. He was also concerned over the anticipated coming of major-league baseball and football to the Twin Cities and the adverse effect it could have on basketball.

Short received approval from the other NBA owners for the move. The Knicks' Ned Irish cast the only dissenting vote, ostensibly because of the added travel expense the teams would incur. Some felt, however, that he was hoping to force the financially-strapped Short to sell Elgin Baylor to the Knicks.

Charlie Johnson was not shy with his opinions regarding the Lakers' failure in Minneapolis. "The downfall of the Lakers," he wrote, "can be summarized as follows: lack of professional leadership and management; mistakes in draft choices, trades, player deals, selection of coaches [he was not referring to Pollard here; undoubtedly he had Castellani in mind], and unwise expenditures; too much switching of games and far too much talk of moving."

Johnson's penultimate point was seconded by Vern

Mikkelsen, who remembered Elgin Baylor arriving late for a game at the Armory because he had gone to the Auditorium, thinking that the game was there. "And it struck me then," said Vern, "if the players don't know where the game is, how can we expect the fans to know?"

Dick Jonckowski, who has maintained contact with many of the Lakers and has organized several reunions of the championship teams, adds, "Many still think the Lakers would be in Minneapolis today had they had an arena they could call home."

City historian Tom Balcom notes that the Lakers couldn't have picked a worse time to have a team in downtown Minneapolis, which was in the midst of a long period of decline. "The high tide of city growth had subsided," said a city planning official of that period, "leaving a backwash of problems which were beyond immediate solution."

Fingers were pointed, bucks were passed—and just as anticipated, Minnesota did get major-league baseball and football within the next year, but professional basketball was going to take a vacation from the Twin Cities.

The winning tradition would continue—the Lakers would eventually create another dynasty—but Minneapolis was to be left behind.

The Tradition Continues in Los Angeles

Bob Short was not the only basketball man with an eye on Southern California in the late fifties. Len Corbosiero, a Los Angeles radio producer, had hopes of receiving an NBA expansion franchise to play in the new Los Angeles Sports Arena.

Corbosiero had so much confidence in the area's potential that in 1959 he offered Ben Kerner of the St. Louis Hawks and Eddie Gottlicb of the Philadelphia Warriors huge guarantees to have their teams play a pre-season game in the Sports Arena. Not only would the game be the first major event at the new arena, it would also mark Wilt Chamberlain's debut in the NBA.

As game day neared, however, attention was focused elsewhere. The Los Angeles Dodgers had just beaten the Milwaukee Braves in a tie-breaker playoff series to win the National League pennant. The World Series was coming to the West Coast, and anyone else hoping for much space on the sports page was out of luck.

Corbosiero feared financial ruin, but his faith in the region was justified as over 12,000 fans showed up for the game. Corbosiero hoped that the showing would convince the NBA to grant him a franchise.

Harlem Globetrotters' owner Abe Saperstein was lobbying for the same thing. In the NBA's early years, the struggling league could count on large crowds when it booked games as part of a double-header with the Globetrotters. Saperstein now hoped the NBA moguls would reward him with a Los Angeles franchise.

But the Los Angeles territory would be given to neither Corbosiero nor Saperstein. So piqued was Abe when the league instead allowed the Lakers to move west that he formed an entire league of his own—a new American Basketball League.

Abe Saperstein

The ABL began play in 1961, but lasted only eighteen months. It did produce some interesting features, however. The league extended as far west as Honolulu. To save on travel expenses, visiting teams would play the Hawaii Chiefs four games in a row before leaving the island. The ABL also introduced professional basketball's first black coach: John McLendon of the Cleveland Pipers, which were owned by shipbuilding magnate George Steinbrenner. Another legacy of the league was a three-point field goal for shots taken from beyond twenty-five feet.

Even though this territory was coveted by others, the move could hardly be considered a sure thing for Short and the Lakers, who would keep their nickname even though Los Angeles has as many lakes as

Minneapolis has palm trees. For Short to receive permission for the move, he had to agree to reimburse the other teams for the added travel expenses to the coast. (Part of the cost was offset by having visiting teams play two games in a row in Los Angeles before leaving.)

The Minneapolis Lakers had produced the league's second-worst record in 1959–60; thus, the Lakers would have the second pick in what was to be an outstanding crop of college seniors.

There was no doubt as to who the first player picked would be. Oscar Robertson, a spectacular guard from the University of Cincinnati, would be taken by the Cincinnati Royals. (Part of the Royals' decision to move from Rochester to Cincinnati in 1958 was made in anticipation of insuring themselves the territorial draft rights to Robertson.)

The Lakers would have their choice of another guard, Jerry West of West Virginia, who was co-captain with Robertson on the U. S. Olympic team, possibly the finest amateur team ever assembled. But also available was center Darrall Imhoff of California. Many felt Imhoff could give the Lakers the type of dominating player in the middle that they hadn't had since the retirement of Mikan. Despite that,

Short drafted West and also signed Jerry's coach at West Virginia, Fred Schaus, as head coach.

Fred Schaus

The Lakers opened training camp in mid-September at Pepperdine University and then played sixteen exhibition games, all of them against the Boston Celtics. The Celtics won twelve games in the preseason series that started in New England and ended in Southern California.

The Los Angeles Sports Arena, scene of the 1960 Democratic National Convention that nominated John Kennedy for president, was to be the Lakers' home. But they would have to share the arena with the UCLA Bruins and the USC Trojans. As a result, many of the dates at the Arena were already booked, and the Lakers were forced to finde alternative playing sites.

The irony of this was not lost on Bob Short's detractors back in the Twin Cities, who howled with laughter when told of his problems at finding arena space in Los Angeles. The game of "musical arenas" that Short thought he was escaping by leaving Minneapolis was continuing to plague him.

They played several games at Los Angeles State

Jerry West

College, and one of their playoff games was played on the huge stage of the antiquated Shrine Auditorium. A highlight of that game was six-eleven Ray Felix, in a scramble for a loose ball, rolling off the stage into the orchestra pit.

The Lakers opened the regular season in Cincinnati, giving ex-Olympic mates Robertson and West the chance to square off in their NBA debuts. Robertson scored twenty-one points and West twenty as the Royals defeated the Lakers, 140–123.

The Lakers' first game in Los Angeles was played five days later before a disappointing crowd of barely 4,000 fans. In fact, Los Angeles would average just over 5,000 in attendance their first year. Good crowds would turn out to see Boston or Philadelphia; for other teams, though, it wasn't until January that a crowd of more than 5,000 arrived.

Schaus broke Jerry West into the lineup gradually. West's playing time increased as the season wore on and by the end of the year, he had become "Mr. Outside," the perfect complement to "Mr. Inside," Elgin Baylor.

As for Elgin, he finished second to Wilt Chamberlain in scoring, with a 34.8 average highlighted by an incredible performance against the Knicks in Madison Square Garden in mid-November, when he scored seventy-one points, breaking his own league record of sixty-four.

With a regular-season record of 36–43, the Lakers finished second to the St. Louis Hawks, who had one of the highest scoring front lines in history, with Clyde Lovellette flanked by Bob Pettit and Cliff Hagan. Even so, the Lakers pushed the Hawks to the limit in the playoffs.

The Hawks, after losing three of the first five games, escaped elimination in Game Six as Pettit's basket in overtime gave St. Louis a 114–113 win. In the seventh game, the Lakers blew a thirteen-point lead, and the Hawks pulled out a 105–103 win.

There was reason for optimism, however. Seats at the Sports Arena were finally becoming scarce. A record crowd of 14,841 came out for their final home playoff game. Even so, Short had to buy his own radio time for the playoffs and hire his own announcers, one of whom was Chick Hearn. It was to be the start of a long marriage between the team and the man who would become known as "The Voice of the Lakers." In addition to his play-by-play duties, Hearn would eventually become an assistant general manager for the Lakers.

The 1961–62 season had just started when President Kennedy activated Army Reserve and National Guard units in response to the Soviet Union's erection of the Berlin Wall. One of those affected by this Soviet construction activity was Elgin Baylor, who was called up for military duty. Using his weekend passes, Baylor managed to play in forty-eight games during the regular season, although he hoarded his leave time for April so he could be available for the playoffs.

When he wasn't toting a rifle, Elgin managed a career-high 38.3 points per game. But as impressive as this total was, he was still a distant second to Wilt Chamberlain, who averaged 50.4 points, topped by a performance on March 2, 1962 in which he scored 100 points in a game against the Knicks.

With Baylor gone, opposing teams were keying on West, but Jerry still averaged 30.8 points and led the Lakers to first place in the Western Division with a 54–26 record, the team's first winning season since the retirement of Jim Pollard.

The Lakers made it to the championship round of the playoffs against the Celtics and split the first two games in Boston. They then took the lead in the series with an incredible finish in Game Three.

The Lakers trailed by four as the game entered its final minute. West's jumper closed the gap to two with thirty-one seconds left. Los Angeles got the ball back, and Jerry converted a pair of free throws to tie the score with three seconds on the clock. Boston called time out in order to inbound the ball from midcourt. But Sam Jones's pass never reached Bob Cousy, its intended target. Instead, West intercepted, drove toward the basket and laid in the winning field goal just ahead of the buzzer.

The Celtics won the next game to tie the series, but the Lakers again grabbed the lead with a win in the fifth game at Boston Garden as Baylor scored sixty-one points, a playoff record that stood until 1986 when it was broken by the Chicago Bulls' Michael Jordan in a double-overtime game. The Celtics staved off elimination by winning Game Six on the Lakers' home court, and the series came down to a seventh game in Boston.

Just as they had in the third game, the Lakers trailed by four points with under a minute remaining. This time it was Frank Selvy who would tie the game with consecutive field goals. After a Boston miss, the Lakers rebounded and called time out with five seconds left.

Selvy inbounded the ball to Hundley at the top of the key. Hot Rod looked to his right, but K. C. Jones had broken through Rudy LaRusso's screen and had West covered. Instead, Hundley bounced a pass to Selvy on the left baseline. With Cousy rushing to cover, Selvy put up a shot with three seconds left. As the ball sailed through the air, the outcome of the NBA championship was out of the hands of mortals.

The ball hit the near edge of the rim and caromed across the hoop. A sudden jolt of gravity at that time and the Lakers would be world champs. But Newton's discovery was not present in sufficient force, and the ball glided across the open hole, struck the far rim, and fell off into the hands of Bill Russell (one of forty rebounds he would snare in the game) as the buzzer signalled the end of regulation play.

Selvy's shot was as close as the Lakers would come. Boston outscored them in overtime to capture the title, their fourth straight, breaking the record of three-in-a-row held by the Minneapolis Lakers.

The Lakers exuded a "Wait Until Next Year" attitude, but they didn't know yet that this series with the Celtics would be the first in a long line of near misses that would earn them the title of basketball's Most Frustrated Team.

In 1962–63 the Lakers won the Western Division title again despite losing Jerry West for twenty-four games with a hamstring tear at mid-season and despite the presence of Wilt Chamberlain in their division.

Eddie Gottlieb had sold the Philadelphia Warriors to a group of men who moved the team to San Francisco. The Warriors transferred to the Western Division and the Cincinnati Royals shifted to the East. But even though Chamberlain led the NBA in both scoring and rebounding and teammate Guy Rodgers topped the league in assists, the Warriors finished a distant fourth and missed the playoffs.

The Lakers found themselves in a rematch with Boston in the championship round. This year, however, it was no contest. Boston won the first two games and three of the first five.

The Celtics wrapped it up in Game Six at the Sports Arena. Boston held a nine-point lead early in the fourth quarter when Bob Cousy, who had announced that he would retire at the end of the season, twisted his ankle and went to the bench. The Lakers rallied and closed the gap to one point with 4:20 to go, when Cousy came limping back onto the court.

The game stayed close through the final minutes, but the Celtics held on for a 112–109 win. Cousy dribbled out the final seconds of his career and flung the ball toward the ceiling in exaltation as time expired, and the Celtics had their fifth-straight championship.

The Lakers didn't even make it beyond the opening round of the playoffs in 1964. The San Francisco Warriors, with the addition of six-eleven Nate Thurmond to reinforce Chamberlain, bounced back to win the division and advance to the final round before falling to the Celtic juggernaut.

Jim Krebs retired prior to the opening of the 1964–65 season. The six-eight center from Southern Methodist had been with the Lakers since 1957, but never lived up to the fanfare that had earned him the nickname "Incredible" Krebs. Krebs would die in a freak accident less than a year later when a heavy branch fell on him as he was helping a neighbor cut down a tree. To fill his spot in the pivot, the Lakers acquired Darrall Imhoff, the center they had passed on in the 1960 draft.

The Lakers won their division in 1965, but lost Elgin Baylor, who shattered his kneecap in the opening playoff round. Baylor would recover and come back the following year, but would never be the same freewheeling player that he once was.

As Baylor underwent surgery on his knee, the Lakers advanced and prepared for the championship round without him. Meanwhile, attention was focused on a ferocious playoff series for the Eastern title between the Celtics and the Philadelphia 76ers (nee Syracuse Nationals). The 76ers had been bolstered by the mid-season acquisition of Wilt Chamberlain, who returned to his hometown in a trade with the Warriors. Wilt led his new team to a seventh-game showdown with Boston and nearly knocked off the champs.

The Celtics had a one-point lead and possession of the ball out of bounds with five seconds left. But Russell's attempted pass in struck the guide wire supporting the backboard, and the ball turned over to Philadelphia, who would have one final chance to win. But that chance was denied when the Celtics' John Havlicek stepped in front of Hal Greer's inbound pass and deflected it to Sam Jones, who dribbled out the remaining seconds.

After that, the playoff finals against the Baylor-less Lakers were anticlimactic. West tried to carry the

Jerry West and Elgin Baylor were an unstoppable duo for the Lakers in the 60s

load alone, and, although he set a record by averaging over forty points per game in the playoffs, Los Angeles was no match for the Celtics, who won the championship series in five games.

Jerry West lays in two of the 25,192 points he would score in his career

The Lakers would be under new ownership by the time the 1965–66 season opened. Bob Short, who had become the sole owner after buying out the other stockholders shortly after the team had moved to Los Angeles, was ready to sell out himself. The price tag on the Lakers was $5,175,000, a phenomenal sum considering that the sale price of the Philadelphia Warriors in 1962 had been $850,000. In only three years, the value of an NBA franchise had quintupled.

Short had continued to live in Minneapolis even after the team moved and, starting in 1961, had brought the Lakers back for a regular-season game at the Minneapolis Auditorium each year. Short was to return to sports, this time baseball, in 1968 when he purchased the Washington Senators, another team he would uproot and move within a few years. He also tried his hand at politics, but was an unsuccessful candidate for Minnesota Lieutenant Governor in the sixties, and was defeated in a 1978 bid for the late Hubert Humphrey's U. S. Senate seat. Short died of cancer in 1982.

The new boss of the Lakers was a native Canadian who had made his fortune in publishing and the fledgling cable television industry. Jack Kent Cooke had previously owned a minor-league baseball team — the Toronto Maple Leafs of the International League — and held a 25% interest in the Washington Redskins football team. He had been unsuccessful in landing the American League baseball expansion team in Los Angeles; instead, he would settle for an NBA franchise.

Slowly during the 1965–66 season, Baylor returned to full strength, and the Lakers captured their fourth regular-season Western Division title in five years. After disposing of the St. Louis Hawks in the preliminary playoff round, they advanced to the final round for another shot at the NBA championship.

It appeared that they might have a different opponent this year. Boston had been unseated in the East by Philadelphia, the first time since the coming of Bill Russell that the Celtics had failed to finish first in their division during the regular season. But in the playoffs they beat the 76ers and would now try for another league title in what would be the farewell for Red Auerbach as coach of the Celtics.

The Lakers took the opening game, but Auerbach stole the headlines by announcing his successor — Bill Russell, who would become player-coach the following season.

Jack Kent Cooke

79

The Celtics took the following three games, but the Lakers roared back to win the next two and force a seventh game at the Boston Garden.

With the Celtics holding an eight-point lead with fifteen seconds left in the game, Auerbach felt safe in lighting his traditional victory cigar. He almost swallowed it, though, as the Lakers reeled off six points before the final buzzer sounded. But the Celtics held on for a 95–93 win and their eighth-straight NBA title.

Time runs out on the Lakers as fans prepare to swarm onto the floor of the Boston Garden in celebration of the Celtics' eighth-consecutive championship

Neither the Celtics nor the Lakers were to find themselves in the championship round in 1967. In the East, the 76ers knocked off Boston, first by finishing the regular season with a mark of 68–13 for a record .840 winning percentage, then by polishing off the Celtics in five games in the playoffs. The new champions of the Western Division were the San Francisco Warriors, under first-year coach Bill Sharman. Led by Nate Thurmond and Rick Barry, who had unseated Chamberlain as the league scoring champion, the Warriors won their division by five games, then defeated the Lakers and St. Louis in the playoffs before falling to Chamberlain and the 76ers for the NBA championship.

But the Lakers and the Celtics would bounce back and meet in the finals the next two years—a familiar scene which would have familiar results.

Los Angeles did have a new face on the bench, however. Fred Schaus had been elevated to general manager and replaced as coach by ex-Marine Bill (Butch) van Breda Kolff, who had been a charter

member of the New York Knicks in 1946. van Breda Kolff had compiled a 103–31 record the previous five seasons as basketball coach at Princeton; prior to that he had coached for seven years at Hofstra University.

The Lakers also had a new home. When Jack Kent Cooke had been granted the Los Angeles Kings' expansion franchise in the National Hockey League, he promised the NHL Board of Governors that he would build his own arena to house both the Kings and the Lakers. On New Years' Eve of 1967 the Lakers played their first game in the Forum in Inglewood. The Fabulous Forum (Cooke instructed his staff in a memo to never say the word Forum without prefacing it with that adjective) was Greek in style and had eighty columns, each fifty-seven feet high, forming the arcade around the building. The structure cost more than seventeen million dollars and the land on which it stood four million—all paid for with private funds.

Snug in their new castle, the Lakers won thirty of their final thirty-eight games to finish second in the West behind St. Louis (the Warriors dropped to third as Rick Barry left the team to sign a contract with the Oakland Oaks of the new American Basketball Association).

But the Hawks were upset in the opening playoff round by the Warriors, who were then swept in the semi-final round by Los Angeles, earning the Lakers another shot at the Celtics in the championship round.

Boston won two of the first three games. In Game Four van Breda Kolff was ejected by referee Mendy Rudolph after drawing two technical fouls, and guard Gail Goodrich took over the coaching duties. The Lakers won the game, 118–105, but Goodrich, trying to concentrate on both playing and coaching, neglected to remove some of the starters after the game was locked up. It was an oversight that became costly when, in the final minute, Jerry West collided with John Havlicek while diving for a loose ball and sprained his ankle.

It was doubtful as to whether West would be able to play in the fifth game. But, not only did he play, he scored thirty-five points, including the tying basket in the final minute of regulation play. The Celtics won the game, however, in overtime to take a three-game-to-two lead in the series.

Back at the Forum in Game Six, John Havlicek scored forty points to lead the Celtics to a 124–109 win and their tenth championship in twelve years. For the Lakers, the frustration continued.

The Fabulous Forum

Tired of being snake-bit, Jack Kent Cooke went shopping in the summer of 1968. Ever since the retirement of George Mikan, the Lakers had lacked a dominating center. A long list of pivotmen had tried to fill the middle since the mid-fifties – Clyde Lovellette, Lew Hitch, Walter Dukes, Jim Krebs, Larry Foust, Ray Felix, Leroy Ellis, Gene Wiley, Jim (Bad News) Barnes, Erwin Mueller, Darrall Imhoff – but now a center was available who could make the Lakers heavy favorites to win the NBA title.

Wilt Chamberlain made it known that he wanted to leave Philadelphia and come to Southern California, setting off a series of cloak-and-dagger negotiations.

While Cooke and 76er owner Irv Kosloff talked of a possible trade, George Mikan, Commissioner of the one-year-old American Basketball Association, was trying to land Wilt for his league. All eleven teams of the ABA contributed to a multi-million dollar contract for Chamberlain to play for the Los Angeles Stars.

In the end, though, Chamberlain opted to stay in the NBA, and the Lakers sent Jerry Chambers, Darrall Imhoff, and Archie Clark to Philadelphia in exchange for him. Most pundits conceded the title to the team that could now put Wilt Chamberlain, Jerry West, and Elgin Baylor on the same floor.

*A 1968 trade which brought Wilt Chamberlain to Los Angeles
made the Lakers strong favorites to win the NBA
championship*

It would not be that easy, however. Gail Goodrich had been taken by the Phoenix Suns in the expansion draft. And in trading Archie Clark, who had averaged 19.9 points per game the year before, to the 76ers, West was left without a suitably dangerous partner in the backcourt, a situation he had never before faced.

And coordinating play between the stars would be

Former Minnesota Gopher star Archie Clark was among a group of players trade for Wilt Chamberlain.

Gail Goodrich helped UCLA win national basketbal titles in 1964 and 1965 before joining the Lakers.

a challenge, as well. West worked from the outside; the presence of Chamberlain would pose no problem for him. But Baylor was Mr. Inside, and the addition of Wilt could create congestion in the lane, where Elgin operated at his best. To open up the middle, Chamberlain was moved to the high post, which left him out of position for rebounding and, in his words, "feeling like a first baseman trying to play centerfield."

This was only one of many disagreements that developed between Chamberlain and van Breda Kolff which led to one of the stormiest years in the history of the Lakers. Not shy in expressing his opinion of his coach, Wilt even claimed that van Breda Kolff eschewed pre-game strategy talks in the locker room and, instead, used the time to stage farting contests.

Chamberlain vs. Russell. Basketball's greatest scorer meets basketball's greatest defender

van Breda Kolff wins the contest

The feud between the men would intensify during the year and reach its peak in the season's final game.

Despite the conflicts, the Lakers still had enough talent to easily win the Western Division and advance through the playoff preliminaries to the championship round. There were upsets in the Eastern Division playoffs, though, and the fourth-place Boston Celtics had survived to represent the East in the finals.

The Lakers won the first two games of the championship series as West hit for fifty-three points in the opener and forty-one points in the second game. Boston won the next game, but trailed in Game Four, 88-87, as the Lakers inbounded the ball with fifteen seconds left.

The Celtics' Emmette Bryant stole the ball, however, and passed to Sam Jones, who took a shot that missed. Chamberlain tipped the rebound to Baylor, who stepped on the baseline trying to control it, and the ball was turned over to Boston again with seven seconds to go.

After a time out, the Celtics inbounded to John Havlicek, who passed to Jones. Sam threw up an off-balance shot, hoping Bill Russell could tap in the rebound (unaware that Russell was no longer in the game). The ball hit the front of the rim, crawled over it, and finally dropped through the basket as the buzzer sounded.

Chamberlain's anguished expression tells the story as Sam Jones's shot wins Game Four for the Celtics

The deadlocked series moved back to Los Angeles. The Lakers won Game Five, 117–104, as Chamberlain outrebounded Russell, 31–13, and outscored him 13–2. West added thirty-nine points, but pulled a hamstring muscle in his left leg in the game's final minutes.

West played in the next game and scored twenty-six points, but Boston won, 99–90, to force a seventh game between the Lakers and Celtics.

This time, the Lakers, by virtue of having a better regular-season record than the Celtics, would have the deciding game at home.

So confident was Cooke of victory that he planned a celebration. Huge nets filled with balloons hung from the rafters of the Forum, to be released at the final buzzer. The USC marching band was standing by, ready to march triumphantly onto the floor playing "Happy Days Are Here Again."

The Celtics were doing their best to halt the festivities, however, and they held a seventeen-point lead with ten minutes to go in the game.

West performed heroically despite the badly-pulled hamstring, and he ended the evening with forty-two points, thirteen rebounds, and twelve assists. Jerry led a Laker comeback, and, with six minutes left, the Celtic lead had shrunk to nine.

Chamberlain grabbed his twenty-seventh rebound of the game a few seconds later, but came down hard on his knee. Play continued as Chamberlain limped up court. Finally, the Lakers called a twenty-second injury timeout, and Wilt hobbled to the bench. His replacement, seven-foot Mel Counts, did a creditable job in relief. Counts hit a ten-foot jumper with three minutes left to cut the margin to one. A few seconds later, Counts hit again, but was called for travelling. The basket was nullified, and the Celtics clung to their 103–102 lead.

Meanwhile, the drama on the bench was rivalling that on the court. Chamberlain signalled van Breda Kolff that he was ready to go back into the game. The coach shook his head. Wilt got up and started for the scorer's table to check in. "Sit down," growled Butch. "We're doing fine without you."

No one will ever know what Chamberlain could have contributed in those frenzied final minutes as Boston managed to hold on for a 108–106 win, their eleventh championship in thirteen years.

The champagne remained corked, the USC band was mute, and the balloons stayed in the rafters as the Laker players, instead of celebrating, had to keep their center and their coach from coming to blows in the locker room.

From that night on, it was obvious that one of the two men would have to go. van Breda Kolff obviated a showdown by resigning to take the head coaching job with the Detroit Pistons. His spot on the Laker bench was taken by a former FBI agent, Joe Mullaney, who had been a college teammate of Bob Cousy's at Holy Cross and had been the coach at Providence College the previous fourteen seasons.

Early into the 1969–70 season Chamberlain suffered the first major injury of his career when he tore the tendons above his right knee. West picked up the slack in scoring during his absence. Even though he was double and triple-teamed with Chamberlain gone, Jerry averaged 31.2 points and was the NBA's top scorer.

The Lakers finished second in the Western Division to the Atlanta Hawks. But Wilt was back for the playoffs, and the Lakers made it to the championship round. Their last obstacle would be the New York Knicks, who had never won an NBA title and were making their first appearance in the final round since 1953.

The teams split the first two games at Madison Square Garden in New York. In Game Three, the Lakers blew a sixteen-point halftime lead, and the score was tied, 100–100, when the Knicks' Dave DeBusschere hit a jumper with three seconds left to give New York a two-point lead. The Lakers were out of time outs, and Chamberlain, from underneath the Knick basket, flipped the ball inbounds to Jerry West and started to walk away. West dribbled three times and, just ahead of the buzzer, fired a shot from just beyond the Knicks' free-throw circle. The shot narrowly missed the scoreboard that hung down from the ceiling, sailed sixty-three feet across the court and into the basket to retie the game. West's heroics, however, would only prolong the game, not win it. The Knicks outscored them, 11–8 in overtime, to take a two-game-to-one lead. But the Lakers won the fourth game, also in overtime, to tie the series again.

Early in Game Five Knicks' center Willis Reed, who would be voted the NBA's Most Valuable Player that season, pulled a muscle in his hip and had to leave the game. New York trailed by thirteen at the half, but even without their center, came back in the second half to win, 107–100.

Reed missed the sixth game, which was won by the Lakers, and his status was uncertain for Game Seven.

Knicks' center Willis Reed went down with a pulled hip muscle in the fifth game of the 1970 championship series

The Knicks came out to warm up before the final game without him. But, just before game time, with the pain in his hip partially numbed by pain-killers, Reed hobbled onto the court, sending the Madison Square Garden crowd into a frenzy.

Reed started the game and got the first two field goals. They were his only points of the night as, physically, he was unable to make much of a difference. Emotionally, though, he already had, and the Knicks rolled to a 113–99 win for their first-ever NBA championship.

In their ten years in Los Angeles, the Lakers had been to the championship round seven times. They had lost every time.

And prospects for bringing a championship to the West Coast were growing dim. True, the Boston Celtics' dynasty had ended (although they wouldn't be down for long), but the Knicks, with Walt Frazier, Willis Reed, Dave DeBusschere, Bill Bradley, and Dick Barnett, had created another powerhouse in the Eastern Conference. And in the West, the Lakers would have to contend with the Milwaukee Bucks, who had just produced the best record ever for a second-year expansion club. The chief reason for the Bucks' success was a seven-foot-two rookie center

from UCLA, Lew Alcindor, who had averaged 28.8 points per game, second in the league to Jerry West.

For the 1970–71 season, the Bucks added Oscar Robertson to their squad and were easily the premier team in the league. They won 66 games to capture first place in the Midwest Division (the NBA now had seventeen teams and had split itself into two conferences and four divisions) and had little trouble in the playoffs getting past the Warriors, Lakers, and Baltimore Bullets to become the NBA champions.

Even though Joe Mullaney had led the Lakers to first place in the Pacific Division, the ex-G-Man was fired at season's end. His replacement would be Bill Sharman, who was on his way to coaching the Utah Stars to the American Basketball Association title.

Sharman was a native of the area and had attended the University of Southern California where as a senior he broke Hank Luisetti's longstanding Pacific Coast Conference scoring record. A standout in basketball and baseball at USC, he continued in both sports following graduation.

Sharman played the outfield for the St. Paul Saints of the American Association in the early fifties. When the 1951 Association season ended, he was called up by the Brooklyn Dodgers, who were in first place in the National League. Sharman was told by manager Charlie Dressen, "We'll put you in the lineup as soon as we clinch the pennant." The Dodgers never clinched, however. They were beaten by Bobby Thomson and the New York Giants in a tiebreaker playoff series, and Sharman never got off the bench.

But Bill spent little time on the bench with the Boston Celtics, where he teamed with Bob Cousy to give the Celts the league's top backcourt duo. Sharman played on four championship teams with the Celtics. Seven times he led the NBA in free-throw percentage, and he retired from the league with a lifetime percentage of .883. He then became a player-coach of the Los Angeles Jets of the American Basketball League in 1961–62. When the Jets folded at midseason, Sharman moved to Cleveland and coached the Pipers to the ABL title. Sharman was named to the NBA Silver Anniversary team in 1970. In 1975 he would be elected to the Basketball Hall of Fame.

Early in the season, the last of the Minneapolis Lakers announced his retirement. Elgin Baylor's knees, which had plagued him since 1963, had carried him as far as they were going to. Baylor had played in only two games the previous year. Now,

West, Chamberlain, and Sharman

nine games into the 1971–72 season, he stepped aside. Considered by some to be the most graceful cornerman ever, Baylor was the third leading scorer in league history, with 23,149 points, and the fourth leading rebounder. He had done it all—except for having played on a championship team.

Elgin's last game was October 31, when the Lakers lost to Golden State, 109–105. The added significance of this game was that it would be the Lakers' last loss for more than two months. They played through November and December without a defeat. In the process, they broke Milwaukee's year-old record of twenty-straight wins.

As the victories increased, so did the hoarseness in Bill Sharman's voice. Unlike his predecessors who relied on "freelancing" offenses, Sharman had implemented a comprehensive set of plays. He would call out the appropriate play number, and he also used a voice command to set the defensive strategy. But the constant shouting was putting a severe strain on his larynx and vocal chords.

The Laker winning streak had reached thirty-three when it was finally snapped on January 9 by Alcindor (who by this time had changed his name to Kareem Abdul-Jabbar) and the Bucks.

Still, the loss was only the Lakers' fourth in forty-three games, and they would go on to finish the regular season with a 69–13 record, the best winning percentage ever. In all but one of their eighty-two games, they scored more than 100 points. Near the end of the year they beat the Golden State Warriors, 162–99, setting still another record for the largest margin of victory in NBA history.

During the year, Chamberlain became the first player to score more than 30,000 points in a career. He also took the league rebounding title and passed Bill Russell to become the leading career rebounder. Jerry West led the league in assists for the first time, and he was also the Most Valuable Player in the All-Star Game, played at the Forum, as his last-second basket gave the Western Conference a 112–110 victory.

The Lakers had little trouble sweeping the Chicago Bulls in the opening playoff round. They lost the first game of the semi-final round to Milwaukee, 93–72 (the seventy-two points was the team's lowest total since April 11, 1954), but they won four of the next five to unseat the defending champion Bucks.

Their opponents in the championship round would be the New York Knicks. The Knicks took the first game, but the Lakers won the next three and were on the verge of wrapping it up. The fifth game of the series was set for Sunday afternoon, May 7, at the Forum. Despite playing with a severely sprained wrist and both hands heavily taped, Chamberlain scored twenty-four points. His padded paws pulled down twenty-nine rebounds and the Lakers surged to a 114–110 victory.

For the first time, the Los Angeles Lakers were champions of the world.

The Los Angeles Lakers
1971-72 National Basketball Association Champions

Sharman was named Coach of the Year, but it was a costly award. His constant shouting during the season resulted in an ulcerated vocal chord. He was ordered to remain silent for a month.

His voice continued to fade over the next four years. He finally had to give up coaching as polyps on his vocal chords reduced his voice to a whisper, and it eventually deserted him completely. He was made general manager, then president of the Lakers in 1982, a position he held until retiring in 1988.

The Lakers and Knicks made it to the final round again in 1973, but the Knicks turned the tables on Los Angeles, losing the first game but winning the next four to capture the championship.

This would be the last appearance of the Lakers in the championship round in the seventies. It would also be the end of the Chamberlain era. After setting an NBA record with a .727 field-goal percentage in 1972–73 (he is still the only man to shoot over 70 percent from the field for an entire season), Wilt retired as a player to become coach of the ABA San Diego Conquistadors.

Following Chamberlain's departure, the Lakers missed the playoffs the next two years and dropped all the way to the cellar in the Pacific Division with the second-worst record in the entire league in 1974–75.

The search for a big man in the middle was on again, and the Lakers filled the void in the summer of 1975. After six seasons in Milwaukee, seven-foot-two Kareem Abdul-Jabbar decided he wanted a change of scenery and asked the Bucks to trade him. Abdul-Jabbar's first choice was to return to his hometown of New York, but when a trade between the Bucks and the Knicks could not be worked out, Kareem agreed instead to come back to of Los Angeles, site of his college career with UCLA, and a trade between the Bucks and Lakers was consummated.

Kareem had already been named the NBA's Most Valuable Player three times while with the Bucks. With the Lakers, he would win the award three more times.

Abdul-Jabbar led the league in rebounding his first year in Los Angeles and helped the Lakers improve their record by ten games in 1975–76, but the team still finished fourth in the Pacific Division and missed the playoffs.

Jerry West, who retired as a player following the 1974 season, returned as coach in 1976 and produced winning records, including one divisional title, in his three years on the bench. But the Lakers were knocked off in preliminary playoff rounds each year.

The Lakers would have a different look all around in 1979: in the front office, on the bench, and on the floor.

The team changed ownership for the third time in its history. Jerry Buss, a former ditch digger from Wyoming who had come to California and made his fortune in real estate, swapped investments with Jack Kent Cooke. Cooke gave up a basketball and a hockey franchise, the Lakers and the Kings, as well as the Fabulous Forum, in exchange for several of Buss's properties, including the Chrysler Building in New York.

A 1975 trade brought Kareem Abdul-Jabbar back to southern California.

Cooke's final decision as owner was how to use the Lakers' first draft choice, which would be the number-one pick overall in the league (the Lakers had received the New Orleans Jazz's 1979 first-round choice as compensation for New Orleans's signing of Laker free-agent Gail Goodrich three years earlier.) Cooke used it to select a nineteen-year-old guard who had just completed his sophomore year at Michigan State, Earvin (Magic) Johnson.

Magic Johnson was the first player taken in the 1979 college draft.

Buss's first major decision was to select a new coach. West, deciding he did not enjoy coaching, was moved upstairs and eventually made general manager. As a successor to West, Buss named Jack McKinney, the former head coach at St. Joseph's College in Philadelphia and a longtime assistant coach in the NBA.

Under McKinney, the Lakers won nine of their first thirteen games of the 1979–80 season. But in early November McKinney was involved in a near-fatal bicycle accident. He survived, but suffered a concussion as well as several broken bones. Assistant Paul Westhead took over as acting coach while McKinney struggled to recover from his injuries.

Paul Westhead

Westhead was eventually made permanent head coach, and he guided the team to its first appearance in the championship round in seven years. The Lakers held a three-game-to-two lead over the 76ers in the series, but were travelling to Philadelphia for Game Six without Kareem Abdul-Jabbar, the league's Most Valuable Player that season.

Kareem was grounded with a sprained ankle and was staying home in hopes of being sufficiently recovered to be able to play in Game Seven. A seventh game would not be necessary, however. Magic John-

son capped his rookie season by moving from guard to center and scoring forty-two points while adding fifteen rebounds and seven assists. Even without Abdul-Jabbar, the Lakers outrebounded Philadelphia and won the game to capture their second NBA championship since moving to Los Angeles.

In the eighties, the wait between titles would not be as lengthy. They were back in the championship round two years later under yet another new coach.

Paul Westhead had fallen into disfavor with Buss, and with some of his players, early in the 1981–82 season because of a new offense he had implemented, a complicated system which called for more picks and moves and allowed for little freewheeling. "This offense is not working," said Buss. "I'm disappointed in not seeing an exciting team once again." And on November 19, even though the Lakers had won seven of their first eleven, Westhead was fired.

His dismissal came a day after he had been blasted by Magic Johnson, who was quoted as saying, "I haven't been happy all season, and I'm not happy now. I can't play here anymore. I want to leave. I want to be traded."

Buss said that Johnson's outburst was unfortunate in its timing, but that it had nothing to do with his decision to fire Westhead; nevertheless, newspaper headlines such as "New Magic trick: Johnson makes coach vanish" were typical.

First reports concerning a successor to Westhead indicated that the Lakers were going to use a unique dual-coach set-up with Jerry West heading the offense and Pat Riley handling the defense. West, however, stayed off the bench, and the coaching was done solely by Riley.

Riley had played nine seasons in the NBA, including five with the Lakers. After retiring in 1976 he joined Chick Hearn in the Laker broadcast booth. When Westhead replaced Jack McKinney as coach in 1979, Riley became an assistant coach. Now, he would succeed Westhead as head coach.

The Lakers won eleven of their next thirteen games and went on to win the Pacific Division by five games over Seattle. They then swept Phoenix and San Antonio in the playoffs to advance to the finals and another meeting with the 76ers.

The Lakers won the championship series opener for their ninth-straight playoff win, tying a league record set by the Minneapolis Lakers in 1949 and 1950.

Pat Riley

Philadelphia fell in six games, and the Lakers had their second championship in three years. Magic Johnson had thirteen points, thirteen rebounds, and thirteen assists in the final game and was named the Most Valuable Player of the championship series.

The Lakers had not only won the 1982 NBA title, but they would have the first pick in the college draft, thanks to a trade they had made with the Cleveland Cavaliers in 1980. They used their choice to select North Carolina forward James Worthy, who had just completed his junior season by leading the Tar Heels to the NCAA title.

The Lakers and 76ers would compete for the NBA title again in 1983, but by this time the Sixers had some additional ammunition. Just prior to the opening of the 1982–83 season, they acquired center Moses Malone in a trade with Houston.

Malone had been the NBA's Most Valuable Player the previous year. In his first year with the 76ers he led the league in rebounding and won the MVP award again.

After adding Malone to a lineup that already had Julius Erving, who was thirty-two years old but could still soar, Philadelphia had little trouble posting the league's best regular-season record and advancing to the championship round.

Fully healthy, the Lakers would have had a tough time with the 76ers. But, entering the final playoff round, they were without Worthy, who had broken his leg in the final week of the regular season. With forward Bob McAdoo and guard Norm Nixon also ailing, the Lakers were no match for Philadelphia, who swept the series in four games.

The Lakers made it back to the championship round in 1984 and faced the Boston Celtics in the first post-season meeting between the two teams since 1969. The series would also feature another championship battle between Magic Johnson and the Celtics' Larry Bird. They had first met their final year in college when Johnson's Michigan State team beat Bird and Indiana State for the 1979 NCAA championship.

The Lakers won two of the first three games of the series against the Celtics. Abdul-Jabbar had thirty-two points in the opener, and Johnson recorded twenty-one assists in a Game Three win. But after six games the series was even, with two of the Boston victories coming in overtime.

In the deciding seventh game in Boston, the Celtics cruised to a 111–102 win as Bird was named the series MVP.

Including their years in Minneapolis, the Lakers had now met the Celtics for the NBA title eight times. Each meeting ended with another championship banner hanging in Boston Garden.

But the Lakers would have another chance in 1985. They won the Pacific Division by twenty games over Portland, their next nearest rival, and had little trouble disposing of Phoenix, Portland, and Denver in the preliminary playoff rounds en route to another rendezvous with the Celtics.

The Lakers survived a 148–114 drubbing in the first game and battled to a three-game-to-two lead as the series moved back to the Boston Garden for Game Six. Magic Johnson responded with a triple-double: fourteen points, fourteen assists, ten rebounds. Abdul-Jabbar added twenty-nine points and Worthy twenty-eight. At the final buzzer the score was Los Angeles 111, Boston 100. The Lakers had beaten the Celtics, and more than two decades of frustration was at an end.

The National Basketball Association championship cup, an award in which the name LAKERS has been engraved often.

The Lakers got off to another fast start in 1985–86, winning twenty-four of their first twenty-seven. They had no trouble finishing first in the Pacific Division again, this time by twenty-two games over second-place Portland.

Los Angeles breezed past San Antonio in the opening playoff round. They then finished off Dallas in six games. Now only the Houston Mavericks stood between the Lakers and their fifth-straight trip to the championship series. On the third leg of their march through Texas, however, they stumbled.

The Lakers beat the Rockets in the opening game, but dropped the next four and were denied another shot at the Boston Celtics.

But that chance would come again. In 1986–87 Magic Johnson, who averaged 23.9 points per game and a league-leading 12.2 assists, was voted the NBA's Most Valuable Player. Behind Magic, the Lakers produced the league's best regular-season record, then won eleven of twelve games in the preliminary playoff rounds to win the Western Conference title and earn themselves another berth in the championship series against the Celtics.

The Lakers won the first two games of the series at home. Back in Boston, though, the Celtics captured Game Three, and they held a 106–105 lead in the closing seconds of the fourth. But with two seconds left, Magic Johnson completed a drive from the left sideline to the lane with a running hook shot that fell through the basket from ten feet away. The Celtics called time out and had one final chance, but Larry Bird's shot from the corner was no good, and the Lakers had opened up a three-game-to-one lead in the series.

Boston avoided elimination with a win in the fifth game, but the Lakers wrapped it up back at the Forum with a 106–93 win in Game Six. Johnson averaged 26.2 points and thirteen assists per game and was named the MVP of the championship series.

It was the Lakers' second championship in three years and their fourth title of the eighties. But it wasn't good enough for Pat Riley, who boldly announced that he was "guaranteeing" another championship for 1988. If the Lakers could back up their coach's brash prediction, they would become the first team to win back-to-back titles since the Celtics did it in 1968 and 1969.

Forty-year-old Kareem Abdul-Jabbar began his nineteenth year in the league by helping the Lakers win their first eight games of the 1987–88 season.

Los Angeles then dropped six out of their next nine games, but snapped out of their slump with a 115–114 victory in Boston on Magic Johnson's running, twenty-foot, one-handed bank shot at the buzzer. The dramatic win over the Celtics was also the first in what was to become a fifteen-game winning streak, the second longest in Laker history.

They finished the regular season with their seventh-consecutive Pacific Division title and again posted the best record in the league.

The Lakers beat San Antonio in three straight in the opening playoff round, but then the road got rock-ier. They were stretched to the limit by the upstart Utah Jazz, but finally won the series in seven games. The battle for the Western Conference championship also came down to a seventh game, but the Lakers prevailed with a 117–102 victory over the Dallas Mavericks.

Their final roadblock would be the Detroit Pistons, who were making their first appearance in the championship round since 1956, when they were still in Fort Wayne. The only league championships ever won by the Pistons were in 1945 and 1946, when they were members of the National Basketball League. (They also won the World Pro Basketball Tournament in 1944, 1945, and 1946.)

Detroit had never won an NBA title, but found themselves on the verge of doing so when they won three of the first five games against the Lakers and held a three-point lead with a minute left in Game Six.

But Byron Scott hit a seventeen-foot jumper for the Lakers to cut the lead to one. Isiah Thomas, who had scored forty-three points in the game for the Pistons, then missed a shot from the left corner. Worthy rebounded and the Lakers called time out to set up a play.

The strategy was to go to Abdul-Jabbar. Kareem set up on his favorite spot on the baseline, got the ball, wheeled, and unleashed his skyhook. The shot hit the rim and bounced away, but Abdul-Jabbar was fouled by Bill Laimbeer. With fourteen seconds to go, Kareem stepped to the line and converted both free throws and the Lakers recorded a 103–102 victory.

The Lakers fell behind again in the seventh and deciding game. They trailed 52–47 at halftime, but connected on their first ten shots of the third quarter to open up an eleven-point lead. With James Worthy, who would end the evening with thirty-six points, sixteen rebounds, and ten assists, leading the charge, they increased the lead to 94–79 with 7:24 left in the game.

Detroit rallied, however, and closed the gap to two points with just under three minutes to go. But that was as close as they would get as the Lakers held on for a 108–105 win, their second-straight championship and their fifth title of the 1980s.

Would he "guarantee" another championship, Riley was asked in the locker room after the game. Abdul-Jabbar promptly stuffed a towel in his coach's mouth.

For Kareem, the 1988–89 season would be his last.

In his three years at UCLA, Lew Alcindor led the Bruins to three NCAA titles. In this game against the Minnesota Gophers, Alcindor blocks a shot by Larry Mikan, son of another Laker legend.

He was born Ferdinand Lewis Alcindor, Jr. in Harlem on April 16, 1947. After leading his high-school team at Power Memorial Academy to a four-year record of 95–6, including a seventy-one game winning streak, he became the subject of one of the greatest recruiting battles ever. Colleges from across the country, even schools with all-white teams, were at his doorstep. Said one coach from the South, "Get me Alcindor and I'll integrate. They'll forget his color when he makes us national champions."

He picked UCLA and scored fifty-six points in his first varsity game for John Wooden's Bruins. UCLA cruised to an 88–2 record during Alcindor's three seasons and won the NCAA championship each year. Alcindor was named college Player of the Year his sophomore and senior years (he was runner-up to Houston's Elvin Hayes his junior year) and was the NCAA tournament Outstanding Player each year. So awesome was he that, following his sophomore season, the NCAA banned the dunk shot.

Drafted by the Milwaukee Bucks in the NBA and the New York Nets in the ABA, he chose Milwaukee and was named the league's Rookie of the Year. The next year, he helped lead the Bucks to the NBA title and won his first of six Most Valuable Player awards. This year, 1971, he also changed his name to Kareem Abdul-Jabbar.

He came to the Lakers, along with Walt Wesley, in a June 16, 1975 trade for Elmore Smith, Brian Winters, and the draft rights to Dave Meyers and Junior Bridgeman.

When he played he his final regular-season game fourteen years later, he was the NBA's all-time leader in seasons (20), points (38,387), games (1,560), minutes played (57,446), field goals made (15,837), field goals attempted (28,307), blocked shots (3,189), and personal fouls (4,657).

He had led the league in scoring twice, rebounding once, played in nineteen All-Star games, and was named to the NBA 35th Anniversary All-Time team in 1980.

The Lakers won their last five regular-season games in 1989 to finish two games ahead of the Phoenix Suns in the Pacific Division. Magic Johnson won his second Most Valuable Player award, narrowly edging out Chicago's Michael Jordan.

Los Angeles finished off Portland in three-straight games in the opening playoff round, and then swept Seattle in four, winning the final game after overcoming a twenty-nine point Sonic lead.

They received a tougher battle from the Phoenix Suns in the Western Conference final. The Lakers' average margin of victory was only five-and-a-half points per game, but it was still enough for another series sweep.

They had now won eleven-straight games in the 1989 playoffs; counting their final two victories against Detroit the year before, their playoff winning streak stood at thirteen, easily breaking their own league record.

Meanwhile, in the Eastern Conference final, the Pistons were locked in a struggle with the surprisingly-stubborn Chicago Bulls, a team which had produced only the sixth-best record in the East. The Bulls took a two-game-to-one lead, helped by a forty-six point performance by Michael Jordan in Game Three, but the Pistons won the final three games to earn another shot at the Lakers.

Detroit had been the NBA's second-best defensive team, allowing opponents only 100.8 points per game during the season; in the playoffs, they had yet to give up 100 points in a game.

Trouble hit the Lakers even before the championship round began. In practice the day before the first game, Byron Scott tore his left hamstring muscle; he would be lost for the series.

The Lakers suffered their first defeat in more than seven weeks in Game One as the Pistons got off to a fast start and cruised to a 109–97 win.

In the second game, the Lakers grabbed a ten-point lead in the first quarter and held onto a six-point edge at the half. With 4:39 left in the third quarter, however, disaster struck. As a Piston fast break tied the score, 75–75, Magic Johnson grabbed the back of his left leg and pulled up lame.

He had aggravated the hamstring pull that had caused him to miss sixteen games, as well as the All-Star game, at mid-season. While the rest of the players left the court for a time out, Johnson stayed on the floor. He spun away from trainer Gary Vitti, an anguished grimace on his face, not so much from the pain of the hamstring itself, but the pain of knowing he was finished for the game, if not for the rest of the series.

But even with Magic gone, his teammates rebuilt their lead and were ahead by eight at the end of the third quarter. The Pistons, however, scored the first ten points of the final period to take their first lead of the game.

The Lakers' hopes of winning a third-consecutive championship received a setback when Magic Johnson pulled a hamstring muscle in the second game of the championship series.

Detroit increased the margin to seven points before Los Angeles began to battle back. Trailing by two, the Lakers had a chance to tie the game with two seconds left as James Worthy was fouled and stepped to the line. But Worthy sunk only one of the two free throws, and the Pistons escaped with their second win as the series shifted back to Los Angeles.

Magic Johnson started Game Three, but lasted less than five minutes. His replacement, Tony Campbell, scored eleven points, his third consecutive game in double figures, and Kareem Abdul-Jabbar turned in a vintage performance, scoring twenty-four points and grabbing thirteen rebounds.

But their contributions were offset by the Piston's rotating backcourt trio of Joe Dumars, Isiah Thomas, and Vinnie Johnson, who combined for seventy-four points. Dumars, who totaled fifty-five points in the first two games, scored thirty-one more in this one, then preserved the Piston victory by blocking a three-point attempt by David Rivers that could have tied the game in the closing seconds.

Magic Johnson did not even suit up for the fourth game; even with their starting backcourt tandem on the sidelines, however, Los Angeles got off to a 44–28 lead. But the Lakers, after scoring thirty-five points in the first quarter, were held to only sixty-two the rest of the way by the stingy Detroit defense.

The Pistons cut the Lakers lead to six at the half and trailed by two going into the fourth quarter. Worthy scored forty points in the game, but it wasn't enough as the hamstrung Lakers were worn done by Detroit in the final period.

With nineteen seconds to go, and the Pistons holding a seven-point lead, one of the greatest basketball careers ever came to an end. As Kareem Abdul-Jabbar was removed from the game, the 17,505 fans in the Forum rose to pay final tribute to him as a player. The Pistons had already begun to celebrate near their bench, but they paused to join the ovation as Abdul-Jabbar walked off the court for the last time.

The final score was Detroit 105, Los Angeles 97.

For the Pistons, their first NBA title; for the Lakers, the end of an era.

But what an era it had been.

Over the past ten years, the Lakers had produced nine Pacific Division championships as they compiled a 591–229 regular-season record for a .721 winning percentage.

They had been in the championship finals eight of those ten years, and had won five National Basketball Association titles.

They had been clearly established as the team of the 1980s. It was a scene familiar to what it was like when the franchise began forty-two years before.

As for where it had all started, Minneapolis may have been left behind when the Lakers moved west in 1960, but professional basketball continued to surface in the area over the years. In addition to the games the Lakers played at the Minneapolis Auditorium in the early-to-mid 1960s, two other regular-season games were played in the Twin Cities, one between Boston and Detroit in 1966, the other featuring St. Louis and Baltimore in 1967.

And Minnesota got back a team of its own in 1967–68 when the Minnesota Muskies, coached by Jim Pollard, became charter members of the American Basketball Association, an organization that had its league office in Minneapolis and George Mikan as its commissioner.

After averaging only 2,400 fans per game in its first-season, the team was moved to Miami. But another team, the defending ABA-champion Pittsburgh Pipers, moved into replace them. However, fans didn't line up to watch the Minnesota Pipers play either, and, after one season, the team moved back to Pittsburgh.

Over the next twenty years several NBA exhibition games and one ABA regular-season game, as well as a Continental Basketball Association team, the Rochester Flyers, filled in. But in 1989, fans in the state will finally get the real thing again, an NBA team, team when the Minnesota Timberwolves play their first game.

For the Lakers, little remains from the early years when men named Pollard, Mikan, Mikkelsen, and Martin were putting the team name on championship banners and into the history books. But forty years later, history was repeating itself–nineteen-hundred miles from where it had started. Just as the Lakers of the late 40s and early 50s dominated the NBA, the Lakers of the 1980s were still winning world championships.

As Magic Johnson put it, "We are champions and champions never go away."

The winning tradition had come full circle.

Once again, the Lakers had earned the label of dynasty.

THE END OF AN ERA
Kareem Abdul-Jabbar watches the clock tick off the final seconds of his fabulous 20-year NBA career.

Appendix

MINNEAPOLIS LAKERS

1947-48

	G	PTS.	AVG.
George Mikan	56	1195	21.3
Jim Pollard	59	760	12.9
Don Carlson	58	475	8.2
Jack Dwan	55	306	5.6
Herm Schaefer	54	288	5.3
Tony Jaros	58	273	4.7
Don Smith	57	200	3.5
Paul Napolitano	52	155	3.0
Johnny Jorgensen	38	101	2.7
Bill Durkee	23	41	1.8
Bob Gerber	15	36	2.4
Ken Exel	5	4	0.8
Joe Patanelli	5	4	0.8
Jack Rocker	5	4	0.8
Warren Ajax	3	1	0.3
Ted Cook	2	0	0.0

1948-49

	G	PTS.	AVG.
George Mikan	60	1698	28.3
Jim Pollard	53	784	14.8
Herm Schaefer	58	602	10.4
Don Carlson	55	508	9.2
Arnie Ferrin	47	345	7.3
Tony Jaros	59	343	5.8
Jack Dwan	60	276	4.6
Don Forman	44	179	4.1
Meyer (Mike) Bloom	45	126	2.8
Ed (Whitey) Kachan	52	112	2.2
Johnny Jorgensen	48	106	2.2
Earl Gardner	50	89	1.8
Don Smith	8	6	0.8
Jack Tingle	2	2	1.0
Ray Ellefson	3	2	0.7

1949-50

	G	PTS.	AVG.
George Mikan	68	1865	27.4
Jim Pollard	66	973	14.7
Vern Mikkelsen	68	791	11.6
Arnie Ferrin	63	340	5.4
Herm Schaefer	65	330	5.1
Bob Harrison	66	300	4.5
Paul Walther	53	291	5.5
Billy Hassett	60	272	4.5
Slater Martin	67	271	4.0
Don Carlson	57	267	4.7
Tony Jaros	61	240	3.9
Gene Stump	49	163	3.3
Bud Grant	35	91	2.6
Norm Glick	1	2	2.0

1950-51

	G	PTS.	AVG.
George Mikan	68	1932	28.4
Vern Mikkelsen	64	904	14.1
Jim Pollard	54	629	11.6
Slater Martin	68	575	8.5
Bob Harrison	68	401	5.9
Arnie Ferrin	68	352	5.2
Kevin O'Shea	63	271	4.3
Tony Jaros	63	241	3.8
Bud Grant	61	159	2.6
Joe Hutton	60	147	2.5
Ed Beach	12	22	1.8

1951-52

	G	PTS.	AVG.
George Mikan	64	1523	23.8
Vern Mikkelsen	66	1009	15.3
Jim Pollard	65	1005	15.5
Slater Martin	66	616	9.3
Frank (Pep) Saul	61	433	6.8
Bob Harrison	65	401	6.2
Howie Schultz	66	268	4.1
Whitey Skoog	35	234	6.7
Lew Hitch	61	217	3.6
Joe Hutton	60	155	2.6
John Pilch	9	5	0.6

1952-53

	G	PTS.	AVG.
George Mikan	70	1442	20.6
Vern Mikkelsen	70	1047	15.0
Jim Pollard	66	859	13.0
Slater Martin	70	774	10.6
Frank Saul	70	516	7.4
Bob Harrison	70	497	7.1
Jim Holstein	66	266	4.0
Lew Hitch	70	261	3.7
Whitey Skoog	68	250	3.7
Howie Schultz	40	91	2.3

1953-54

	G	PTS.	AVG.
George Mikan	72	1306	18.1
Jim Pollard	71	831	11.7
Vern Mikkelsen	72	797	11.1
Slater Martin	69	684	9.9
Clyde Lovellette	72	588	8.2
Myer (Whitey) Skoog	71	496	7.0
Frank Saul	71	452	6.4
Bob Harrison	64	382	6.0
Dick Schnittker	71	330	4.6
Jim Fritsche	68	281	4.1
Jim Holstein	70	240	3.4

1954–55

	G	PTS.	AVG.
Vern Mikkelsen	72	1327	18.4
Clyde Lovellette	70	1311	18.7
Slater Martin	72	976	13.6
Whitey Skoog	72	785	10.9
Dick Schnittker	72	750	10.4
Jim Pollard	63	681	10.8
Lew Hitch	74	449	6.1
Ed Kalafat	72	347	4.8
Jim Holstein	62	281	4.5
Don Sunderlage	45	114	2.5
Bob Carney	19	69	3.6
Bob Watson	3	18	6.0

1955–56

	G	PTS.	AVG.
Clyde Lovellette	71	1526	21.5
Vern Mikkelsen	72	962	13.4
Slater Martin	72	947	13.2
Whitey Skoog	72	835	11.6
Dick Schnittker	72	812	11.3
Ed Kalafat	72	574	8.0
George Mikan	37	390	10.5
Dick Garmaker	68	388	5.7
Chuck Mencel	69	318	4.6
Lew Hitch	69	288	4.2
Jim Holstein	27	72	2.7
Bob Williams	20	66	3.3
Ron Feiereisel	10	30	3.0
John Horan	19	34	1.8

1956–57

	G	PTS.	AVG.
Clyde Lovellette	69	1434	20.8
Dick Garmaker	72	1177	16.3
Bob (Slick) Leonard	72	792	11.0
Vern Mikkelsen	72	986	13.7
Walter Dukes	71	720	10.1
Chuck Mencel	72	665	9.2
Ed Kalafat	65	553	8.5
Jim Paxson	71	446	6.3
Lew Hitch	68	285	4.2
Whitey Skoog	23	200	8.7
Dick Schnittker	70	386	5.5
Bob Williams	4	4	1.0

1957–58

	G	PTS.	AVG.
Vern Mikkelsen	72	1248	17.3
Larry Foust	72	1210	16.8
Dick Garmaker	68	1094	16.1
Bob Leonard	66	737	11.2
Ed Fleming	72	633	8.8
Jim Krebs	68	533	7.8
Corky Devlin	70	473	6.8
Dick Schnittker	50	457	9.1
Hot Rod Hundley	65	452	7.0
Art Spoelstra	50	382	7.6
Baltico (Bo) Erias	18	148	8.2
Frank Selvy	38	135	3.6
McCoy Ingram	24	67	2.8
Bob Burrow	14	55	3.9
George Brown	1	1	1.0

1958–59

	G	PTS.	AVG.
Elgin Baylor	70	1742	24.9
Vern Mikkelsen	72	992	13.8
Dick Garmaker	72	984	13.7
Larry Foust	72	882	12.3
Rod Hundley	71	682	9.6
Jim Krebs	72	634	8.8
Bob Leonard	58	532	9.2
Ed Fleming	71	461	6.5
Alex (Boo) Ellis	72	428	5.9
Steve Hamilton	67	292	4.4

1959–60

	G	PTS.	AVG.
Elgin Baylor	70	2074	29.6
Rudy LaRusso	71	975	13.7
Rod Hundley	73	933	12.8
Larry Foust	72	877	15.6
Bob Leonard	73	598	8.2
Frank Selvy	62	563	9.1
Tom Hawkins	69	546	7.9
Jim Krebs	75	572	7.6
Dick Garmaker	43	513	11.9
Ray Felix	31	261	8.4
Boo Ellis	46	179	3.9
Ed Fleming	27	171	6.3
Steve Hamilton	15	76	5.1
Bob Smith	10	37	3.7
Nick Mantis	10	21	2.1
Charlie Share	3	7	2.3
Ron Sobiesczyk	1	2	2.0

LOS ANGELES LAKERS

1960-61

	G	PTS.	AVG.
Elgin Baylor	73	2538	34.8
Jerry West	79	1389	17.6
Rudy LaRusso	79	1155	14.6
Rod Hundley	79	869	11.0
Frank Selvy	77	832	10.8
Tom Hawkins	78	760	9.7
Jim Krebs	75	617	8.2
Ray Felix	78	513	6.6
Bob Leonard	55	193	3.5
Howard Jolliff	46	103	2.2
Ron Johnson	14	37	2.6
Gary Alcorn	20	31	1.6

1961-62

	G	PTS.	AVG.
Jerry West	75	2310	30.8
Elgin Baylor	48	1836	38.3
Rudy LaRusso	80	1374	17.2
Frank Selvy	79	1164	14.7
Jim Krebs	78	780	10.0
Tom Hawkins	79	721	9.1
Ray Felix	80	432	5.4
Rod Hundley	78	429	5.5
Howard Jolliff	64	249	3.9
Bob McNeill	50	138	2.8
Wayne Yates	37	72	1.9
Bob Smith	3	0	0.0

1962-63

	G	PTS.	AVG.
Elgin Baylor	80	2719	34.0
Jerry West	55	1489	27.1
Dick Barnett	80	1437	18.0
Rudy LaRusso	75	924	12.3
Frank Selvy	80	826	10.3
Jim Krebs	79	659	8.3
Leroy Ellis	80	577	7.2
Rod Hundley	65	260	4.0
Gene Wiley	75	241	3.2
Ron Horn	28	74	2.6
Howard Jolliff	28	36	1.3

1963-64

	G	PTS.	AVG.
Jerry West	72	2064	28.7
Elgin Baylor	78	1983	25.4
Dick Barnett	78	1433	18.4
Rudy LaRusso	79	972	12.3
Leroy Ellis	78	512	6.6
Don Nelson	80	419	5.2
Frank Selvy	73	398	5.5
Gene Wiley	78	337	4.3
Jim Krebs	68	333	4.9
Jim King	60	234	3.9
Hub Reed	46	76	1.7
Mel Gibson	8	13	1.4

1964-65

	G	PTS.	AVG.
Jerry West	74	2292	31.0
Elgin Baylor	74	2009	27.1
Rudy LaRusso	77	1083	14.1
Dick Barnett	74	1020	13.8
Leroy Ellis	80	820	10.3
Jim King	77	486	6.3
Gene Wiley	80	406	5.1
Darrall Imhoff	76	378	4.8
Walt Hazzard	66	280	4.2
Don Nelson	39	92	2.4
Cotton Nash	25	53	2.1
Bill McGill	8	15	1.9
Jerry Grote	11	14	1.3

1965-66

	G	PTS.	AVG.
Jerry West	79	2476	31.3
Rudy LaRusso	76	1170	15.4
Walt Hazzard	80	1098	13.7
Elgin Baylor	65	1079	16.6
Leroy Ellis	80	972	12.2
Bob Boozer	78	955	12.2
Jim King	76	570	7.5
Gail Goodrich	65	509	7.8
Darrall Imhoff	77	379	4.9
Gene Wiley	67	289	4.3
John Fairchild	30	60	2.0

1966-67

	G	PTS.	AVG.
Jerry West	66	1892	28.7
Elgin Baylor	70	1862	26.6
Gail Goodrich	77	957	12.4
Darrall Imhoff	81	867	10.7
Archie Clark	76	798	10.5
Walt Hazzard	79	731	9.3
Tom Hawkins	76	632	8.3
Rudy LaRusso	45	578	12.8
Jim Barnes	80	562	7.0
Jerry Chambers	68	516	7.6
Mel Counts	31	264	8.5
John Block	22	64	2.9
Henry Finkel	27	41	1.5

1967-68

	G	PTS.	AVG.
Elgin Baylor	77	2002	26.0
Archie Clark	81	1612	19.9
Jerry West	51	1343	26.3
Gail Goodrich	79	1092	13.8
Mel Counts	82	958	11.7
Tom Hawkins	78	903	11.6
Darrall Imhoff	82	763	9.3
Fred Crawford	38	559	8.1
Erwin Mueller	39	325	8.3
Jim Barnes	42	261	6.2
John Wetzel	38	139	3.7
Dennis Hamilton	44	121	2.8
Cliff Anderson	18	26	1.4

1968–69

	G	PTS.	AVG.
Elgin Baylor	76	1881	24.8
Wilt Chamberlain	81	1654	20.5
Jerry West	61	1580	25.9
Mel Counts	77	958	12.4
John Egan	82	696	8.5
Keith Erickson	77	648	8.4
Bill Hewitt	75	539	7.2
Tom Hawkins	74	522	7.1
Fred Crawford	81	505	6.2
Cliff Anderson	35	135	3.9
Jay Carty	28	76	2.7

1969–70

	G	PTS.	AVG.
Jerry West	74	2309	31.2
Elgin Baylor	54	1298	24.0
Happy Hairston	56	1133	21.0
Mel Counts	81	1024	12.6
Dick Garrett	73	846	11.6
Rick Roberson	74	644	8.7
Keith Erickson	68	607	8.9
John Egan	72	529	7.3
Wilt Chamberlain	12	328	27.3
Willie McCarter	40	307	7.7
Mike Lynn	44	119	2.7
John Tresvant	20	117	5.9
Bill Hewitt	20	66	3.3

1970–71

	G	PTS.	AVG.
Jerry West	69	1859	16.9
Wilt Chamberlain	82	1696	20.7
Happy Hairston	80	1485	18.6
Gail Goodrich	79	1380	17.5
Keith Erickson	73	823	11.3
Jim McMillian	81	678	8.4
Willie McCarter	76	540	7.1
Rick Roberson	65	338	5.2
Fred Hetzel	59	282	4.8
Pat Riley	54	266	4.9
John Tresvant	8	43	5.4
Elgin Baylor	2	20	10.0
Earnie Killum	4	1	0.3

1971–72

	G	PTS.	AVG.
Gail Goodrich	82	2127	25.9
Jerry West	77	1985	25.8
Jim McMillian	80	1503	18.8
Wilt Chamberlain	82	1213	14.8
Happy Hairston	80	1047	13.1
Flynn Robinson	64	635	9.9
Pat Riley	67	449	6.7
Leroy Ellis	74	342	4.6
John Q. Trapp	58	329	5.7
Elgin Baylor	9	106	11.8
Jim Cleamons	38	98	2.6
Keith Erickson	15	86	5.7

1972–73

	G	PTS.	AVG.
Gail Goodrich	76	1814	23.9
Jerry West	69	1575	22.8
Jim McMillian	81	1533	18.9
Wilt Chamberlain	82	1084	13.2
Bill Bridges	72	705	9.8
Keith Erickson	76	687	9.0
Happy Hairston	28	456	16.3
Pat Riley	55	399	7.3
Jim Price	59	376	6.4
Mel Counts	59	293	5.0
Travis Grant	33	125	3.8
Bill Turner	19	38	2.0
Flynn Robinson	6	34	5.7
Leroy Ellis	10	26	2.6
John Q. Trapp	5	13	2.6
Roger Brown	1	1	1.0

1973–74

	G	PTS.	AVG.
Gail Goodrich	82	2076	25.3
Jim Price	82	1263	15.4
Happy Hairston	77	1113	14.5
Elmore Smith	81	1015	12.5
Connie Hawkins	71	909	12.8
Pat Riley	72	684	9.5
Jerry West	31	629	20.3
Bill Bridges	65	548	8.4
Stan Love	51	287	5.6
Kermit Washington	45	172	3.8
Mel Counts	45	146	3.2
Nate Hawthorne	33	106	3.2
Travis Grant	3	3	1.0

1974–75

	G	PTS.	AVG.
Gail Goodrich	72	1630	22.6
Lucius Allen	56	1093	19.5
Elmore Smith	74	804	10.9
Brian Winters	68	794	11.7
Happy Hairston	74	759	10.3
Cazzie Russell	40	629	15.7
Stu Lantz	56	523	9.3
Pat Riley	46	507	11.0
Zelmo Beaty	69	380	5.5
Connie Hawkins	43	346	8.0
Corky Calhoun	57	284	5.0
Kermit Washington	55	246	4.5
Stan Love	30	217	7.2
Jim Price	9	191	21.2
Bill Bridges	17	56	3.3

1975-76

	G	PTS.	AVG.
Kareem Abdul-Jabbar	82	2275	27.7
Gail Goodrich	75	1459	19.5
Lucius Allen	76	1119	14.7
Cazzie Russell	74	874	11.8
Don Ford	76	726	9.6
Don Freeman	64	689	10.8
Cornell Warner	81	591	7.3
Corky Calhoun	76	409	5.4
Stu Lantz	53	250	4.7
Kermit Washington	36	123	3.4
Jim McDaniels	35	91	2.6
Cliff Meely	20	64	3.2
Ron Williams	9	44	4.9
C. J. Kupec	16	27	1.7
Pat Riley	2	11	5.5
John Roche	15	8	0.5
Walt Wesley	1	4	4.0

1976-77

	G	PTS.	AVG.
Kareem Abdul-Jabbar	82	2152	26.2
Cazzie Russell	82	1344	16.4
Lucius Allen	78	1139	14.6
Earl Tatum	68	638	9.4
Don Ford	82	597	7.3
Kermit Washington	53	514	9.7
Dwight Lamar	71	502	7.1
Don Chaney	81	496	6.1
Tom Abernethy	70	439	6.3
C. J. Kupec	82	384	4.7
Johnny Neumann	59	346	5.9
Mack Calvin	12	95	7.9
Marv Roberts	28	58	2.1
Cornell Warner	14	54	3.9
Allen Murphy	2	5	2.5

1977-78

	G	PTS.	AVG.
Kareem Abdul-Jabbar	62	1600	25.8
Lou Hudson	82	1123	13.7
Norm Nixon	81	1107	13.7
Adrian Dantley	56	1088	19.4
Jamaal Wilkes	51	660	12.9
Don Ford	79	612	7.7
Charlie Scott	48	560	11.7
Tom Abernethy	73	493	6.8
James Edwards	25	370	14.8
Earl Tatum	25	351	14.0
Kenny Carr	52	323	6.2
Kermit Washington	25	288	11.5
Dave Robisch	55	258	4.7
Ernie DiGregorio	25	98	3.9
Brad Davis	33	82	2.5
Don Chaney	9	31	3.4

1978-79

	G	PTS.	AVG.
Kareem Abdul-Jabbar	80	1903	23.8
Jamaal Wilkes	82	1524	18.6
Norm Nixon	82	1404	17.1
Adrian Dantley	60	1040	17.3
Lou Hudson	78	768	9.8
Ron Boone	82	608	7.4
Kenny Carr	72	533	7.4
Don Ford	79	528	6.7
Dave Robisch	80	386	4.8
Jim Price	75	397	5.3
Ron Carter	46	144	3.1
Brad Davis	5	19	3.8
Michael Cooper	3	6	2.0

1979-80

	G	PTS.	AVG.
Kareem Abdul-Jabbar	82	2034	24.8
Jamaal Wilkes	82	1644	20.0
Norm Nixon	82	1446	17.6
Magic Johnson	77	1387	18.0
Jim Chones	82	869	10.3
Spencer Haywood	76	736	9.7
Michael Cooper	82	722	8.8
Mark Landsberger	23	161	7.0
Don Ford	52	155	3.0
Brad Holland	38	106	2.8
Marty Byrnes	32	63	2.0
Oliver Mack	27	51	1.9
Ron Boone	6	34	5.7
Kenny Carr	5	16	3.2
Butch Lee	11	14	1.3

1980-81

	G	PTS.	AVG.
Kareem Abdul-Jabbar	80	2095	26.2
Jamaal Wilkes	81	1827	22.6
Norm Nixon	79	1350	17.1
Jim Chones	82	882	10.8
Magic Johnson	37	798	21.6
Michael Cooper	81	763	9.4
Mark Landsberger	69	390	5.7
Eddie Jordan	60	306	5.1
Butch Carter	54	301	5.6
Jim Brewer	78	217	2.8
Brad Holland	41	130	3.2
Alan Hardy	22	51	2.3
Myles Patrick	3	5	1.7
Tony Jackson	2	2	1.0

1981-82

	G	PTS.	AVG.
Kareem Abdul-Jabbar	76	1818	23.9
Jamaal Wilkes	82	1734	21.1
Magic Johnson	78	1447	18.6
Norm Nixon	82	1440	17.6
Michael Cooper	76	907	11.9
Bob McAdoo	41	392	9.6
Mitch Kupchak	26	371	14.3
Mark Landsberger	75	321	4.3
Kurt Rambis	64	295	4.6
Eddie Jordan	58	222	3.8
Mike McGee	39	191	4.9
Jim Brewer	71	170	2.4
Kevin McKenna	36	67	1.9
Clay Johnson	7	25	3.6

1982–83

	G	PTS.	AVG.
Kareem Abdul-Jabbar	79	1722	21.8
Jamaal Wilkes	80	1571	19.6
Magic Johnson	79	1326	16.8
Norm Nixon	79	1191	15.1
James Worthy	77	1033	13.4
Bob McAdoo	47	703	15.0
Michael Cooper	82	639	7.8
Kurt Rambis	78	584	7.5
Dwight Jones	32	156	4.9
Mike McGee	39	156	4.0
Clay Johnson	48	144	3.0
Mark Landsberger	39	98	2.5
Eddie Jordan	35	94	2.7
Steve Mix	1	9	9.0
Billy Ray Bates	4	5	1.3
Joe Cooper	2	2	1.0

1983–84

	G	PTS.	AVG.
Kareem Abdul-Jabbar	80	1717	21.5
Jamaal Wilkes	75	1294	17.3
James Worthy	70	1185	14.5
Magic Johnson	67	1178	17.6
Bob McAdoo	70	916	13.1
Byron Scott	74	788	10.6
Mike McGee	77	757	9.8
Michael Cooper	82	739	9.0
Swen Nater	69	311	4.5
Calvin Garrett	41	188	4.6
Kurt Rambis	47	168	3.6
Larry Spriggs	38	124	3.3
Mitch Kupchak	34	104	3.1
Eddie Jordan	3	9	3.0

1984–85

	G	PTS.	AVG.
Kareem Abdul-Jabbar	79	1735	22.0
James Worthy	80	1410	17.6
Magic Johnson	77	1406	18.3
Byron Scott	81	1295	16.0
Mike McGee	76	774	10.2
Michael Cooper	82	702	8.6
Bob McAdoo	66	690	10.5
Larry Spriggs	75	500	6.7
Kurt Rambis	82	430	5.2
Jamaal Wilkes	42	347	8.3
Mitch Kupchak	58	306	5.3
Ronnie Lester	32	89	2.8
Chuck Nevitt	11	12	1.1
Earl Jones	2	0	0.0

1985–86

	G	PTS.	AVG.
Kareem Abdul-Jabbar	79	1846	23.4
James Worthy	75	1500	20.0
Magic Johnson	72	1354	18.8
Byron Scott	76	1174	15.4
Maurice Lucas	77	785	10.2
Michael Cooper	82	758	9.2
Mike McGee	71	587	8.3
A.C. Green	82	521	6.4
Kurt Rambis	74	408	5.5
Mitch Kupchak	55	332	6.0
Larry Spriggs	43	214	5.0
Ronnie Lester	27	67	2.5
Petur Gudmundsson	8	58	7.3
Chuck Nevitt	4	10	2.5
Jerome Henderson	1	4	4.0

1986–87

	G	PTS.	AVG.
Magic Johnson	80	1909	23.9
James Worthy	82	1594	19.4
Byron Scott	82	1397	17.0
Kareem Abdul-Jabbar	78	1366	17.5
Michael Cooper	82	859	10.5
A.C. Green	79	852	10.8
Kurt Rambis	78	446	5.7
Mychal Thompson	33	333	10.1
Billy Thompson	59	332	5.6
Wes Matthews	50	208	4.2
Frank Brickowski	37	146	3.9
Adrian Branch	32	138	4.3
Mike Smrek	35	76	2.2

1987–88

	G	PTS.	AVG.
Byron Scott	81	1754	21.7
James Worthy	75	1478	19.7
Magic Johnson	72	1408	19.6
Kareem Abdul-Jabbar	80	1165	14.6
A.C. Green	82	937	11.4
Mychal Thompson	80	925	11.6
Michael Cooper	61	532	8.7
Wes Matthews	51	289	5.7
Kurt Rambis	70	277	4.0
Milt Wagner	40	152	3.8
Tony Campbell	13	143	11.0
Mike Smrek	48	132	2.8
Ray Tolbert	14	42	3.0
Billy Thompson	9	14	1.6
Jeff Lamp	3	2	0.7

1988–89

	G	PTS.	AVG.
Magic Johnson	77	1730	22.5
James Worthy	81	1657	20.5
Byron Scott	74	1448	19.6
A.C. Green	82	1088	13.3
Kareem Abdul-Jabbar	74	748	10.1
Orlando Woolridge	74	715	9.7
Mychal Thompson	80	738	9.2
Michael Cooper	80	587	7.3
Tony Campbell	63	388	6.2
Mark McNamara	39	113	2.9
David Rivers	47	134	2.9
Jeff Lamp	37	60	1.6

COACHES

Minneapolis Lakers

JOHN KUNDLA

Year	Regular Season W	L	Playoffs W	L
1947–48	43	17	8	2
1948–49	44	16	8	2
1949–50	51	17	11	2
1950–51	44	24	3	4
1951–52	40	26	9	4
1952–53	48	22	9	3
1953–54	46	26	9	4
1954–55	40	32	3	4
1955–56	33	39	2	2
1956–57	34	38	2	4
1957–58	10	23		
1958–59	33	39	6	7
	466	319	70	38

GEORGE MIKAN

Year	Regular Season W	L	Playoffs W	L
1957–58	9	30		

JOHN CASTELLANI

Year	Regular Season W	L	Playoffs W	L
1959–60	11	25		

JIM POLLARD

Year	Regular Season W	L	Playoffs W	L
1959–60	14	25	5	4

Los Angeles Lakers

FRED SCHAUS

Year	Regular Season W	L	Playoffs W	L
1960–61	36	43	6	6
1961–62	54	26	7	6
1962–63	53	27	6	7
1963–64	42	38	2	3
1964–65	49	31	5	6
1965–66	45	35	7	7
1966–67	36	45	0	3
	315	245	33	38

BILL VAN BREDA KOLFF

Year	Regular Season W	L	Playoffs W	L
1967–68	52	30	10	5
1968–69	55	27	11	7
	107	57	21	12

JOE MULLANEY

Year	Regular Season W	L	Playoffs W	L
1969–70	46	36	11	7
1970–71	48	34	5	7
	94	70	16	14

BILL SHARMAN

Year	Regular Season W	L	Playoffs W	L
1971–72	69	13	12	3
1972–73	60	22	9	8
1973–74	47	35	1	4
1974–75	30	52		
1975–79	40	42		
	246	164	22	15

JERRY WEST

Year	Regular Season W	L	Playoffs W	L
1976–77	53	29	4	7
1977–78	45	37	1	2
1978–79	47	35	3	5
	145	101	8	14

JACK MC KINNEY

Year	Regular Season W	L	Playoffs W	L
1979–80	9	4		

PAUL WESTHEAD

Year	Regular Season W	L	Playoffs W	L
1979–80	51	18	12	4
1980–81	54	28	1	2
1981–82	7	4		
	112	50	13	6

PAT RILEY

Year	Regular Season W	L	Playoffs W	L
1981–82	50	21	12	2
1982–83	58	24	8	7
1983–84	54	28	14	7
1984–85	62	20	15	4
1985–86	62	20	8	6
1986–87	65	17	15	3
1987–88	62	20	15	9
1988–89	57	25	11	4
	470	175	98	42

League Standings

National Basketball League
1947–48

Western Division				Eastern Division			
Minneapolis	43 17	.717	—	Rochester	44 16	.733	—
Tri-Cities	30 30	.500	13	Anderson	42 18	.700	2
Oshkosh	29 31	.483	14	Fort Wayne	40 20	.667	4
Indianapolis	24 35	.407	18.5	Toledo	22 37	.373	21.5
Sheboygan	23 37	.383	20	Flint	8 52	.133	36

NBL Champions: Minneapolis Lakers

Basketball Association of America
1948–49

Western Division				Eastern Division			
Rochester	45 15	.750	—	Washington	38 22	.633	—
Minneapolis	44 16	.733	1	New York	32 28	.533	6
Chicago	38 22	.633	7	Baltimore	29 31	.483	9
St. Louis	29 31	.483	16	Philadelphia	28 32	.467	10
Fort Wayne	22 38	.367	23	Boston	25 35	.417	13
Indianapolis	18 42	.300	27	Providence	12 48	.200	26

BAA Champions: Minneapolis Lakers

National Basketball Association
1949–50

Western Division				Eastern Division			
Indianapolis	39 25	.609	—	Syracuse	51 13	.797	—
Anderson	37 27	.578	2	New York	40 28	.588	13
Tri-Cities	29 35	.453	10	Washington	32 36	.471	21
Sheboygan	22 40	.355	16	Philadelphia	26 42	.382	27
Waterloo	19 43	.306	19	Baltimore	25 43	.368	28
Denver	11 51	.177	27	Boston	22 46	.324	31

Central Division			
Minneapolis	51 17	.750	—
Rochester	51 17	.750	—
Fort Wayne	40 28	.588	11
Chicago	40 28	.588	11
St. Louis	26 42	.382	25

NBA Champions: Minneapolis Lakers

1950–51

Western Division				Eastern Division			
Minneapolis	44 24	.647	—	Philadelphia	40 26	.606	—
Rochester	41 27	.603	3	Boston	39 30	.565	2.5
Fort Wayne	32 36	.471	12	New York	36 30	.545	4
Indianapolis	31 37	.456	13	Syracuse	32 34	.485	8
Tri-Cities	25 43	.368	19	Baltimore	24 42	.364	16
				Washington	10 25	.286	14.5

NBA Champions: Rochester Royals

1951–52

Western Division				Eastern Division			
Rochester	41 25	.621	—	Syracuse	40 26	.606	—
Minneapolis	40 26	.606	1	Boston	39 27	.591	1
Indianapolis	34 32	.515	7	New York	37 29	.561	3
Fort Wayne	29 37	.439	12	Philadelphia	33 33	.500	7
Milwaukee	17 49	.258	24	Baltimore	20 46	.303	20

NBA Champions: Minneapolis Lakers

1952–53

Western Division				Eastern Division			
Minneapolis	48 22	.686	—	New York	47 23	.671	—
Rochester	44 26	.629	4	Syracuse	47 24	.662	.5
Fort Wayne	36 33	.522	11.5	Boston	46 25	.648	1.5
Indianapolis	28 43	.394	20.5	Baltimore	16 54	.229	31
Milwaukee	27 44	.380	21.5	Philadelphia	12 57	.174	34.5

NBA Champions: Minneapolis Lakers

1953–54

Western Division				Eastern Division			
Minneapolis	46 26	.639	—	New York	44 28	.611	—
Rochester	44 28	.611	2	Boston	42 30	.583	2
Fort Wayne	40 32	.556	6	Syracuse	42 30	.583	2
Milwaukee	21 51	.292	25	Philadelphia	29 43	.403	15
				Baltimore	16 56	.222	28

NBA Champions: Minneapolis Lakers

1954–55*

Western Division				Eastern Division			
Fort Wayne	43 29	.597	—	Syracuse	43 29	.597	—
Minneapolis	40 32	.556	3	New York	38 34	.528	5
Rochester	29 43	.403	14	Boston	36 36	.500	7
Milwaukee	26 46	.361	17	Philadelphia	33 39	.458	10

NBA Champions: Syracuse Nationals

*The Baltimore Bullets were 3–11 before disbanding on November 27, 1954. The results and statistics of these games were dropped from official league totals.

1955–56

Western Division				Eastern Division			
Fort Wayne	37 35	.514	—	Philadelphia	45 27	.625	—
Minneapolis	33 39	.458	4	Boston	39 33	.542	6
St. Louis	33 39	.458	4	Syracuse	35 37	.486	10
Rochester	31 41	.431	6	New York	35 37	.486	10

NBA Champions: Philadelphia Warriors

1956–57

Western Division	W	L	Pct	GB	Eastern Division	W	L	Pct	GB
St. Louis	34	38	.472	—	Boston	44	28	.611	—
Minneapolis	34	38	.472	—	Syracuse	38	34	.528	6
Fort Wayne	34	38	.472	—	Philadelphia	37	35	.514	7
Rochester	31	41	.431	3	New York	36	36	.500	8

NBA Champions: Boston Celtics

1957–58

Western Division	W	L	Pct	GB	Eastern Division	W	L	Pct	GB
St. Louis	41	31	.569	—	Boston	49	23	.681	—
Detroit	33	39	.458	8	Syracuse	41	31	.569	8
Cincinnati	33	39	.458	8	Philadelphia	37	35	.514	12
Minneapolis	19	53	.264	22	New York	35	37	.486	14

NBA Champions: St. Louis Hawks

1958–59

Western Division	W	L	Pct	GB	Eastern Division	W	L	Pct	GB
St. Louis	49	23	.681	—	Boston	52	20	.722	—
Minneapolis	33	39	.458	16	New York	40	32	.556	12
Detroit	28	44	.389	21	Syracuse	35	37	.486	17
Cincinnati	19	53	.264	30	Philadelphia	32	40	.444	20

NBA Champions: Boston Celtics

1959–60

Western Division	W	L	Pct	GB	Eastern Division	W	L	Pct	GB
St. Louis	46	29	.613	—	Boston	59	16	.787	—
Detroit	30	45	.400	16	Philadelphia	49	26	.653	10
Minneapolis	25	50	.333	21	Syracuse	45	30	.600	14
Cincinnati	19	56	.253	27	New York	27	48	.360	32

NBA Champions: Boston Celtics

Minneapolis Lakers Record Vs.

	Regular Season W	Regular Season L	Playoffs W	Playoffs L
Anderson Packers	5	3	2	0
Baltimore Bullets	*30	7		
Boston Celtics	37	54	0	4
Chicago Stags	8	4	4	0
Denver Nuggets	2	0		
Fort Wayne/Detroit Zollner Pistons	68	60	14	6
Flint Dow Chemicals	5	1		
Indianapolis Kautskys/Jets	11	1		
Indianapolis Olympians	19	12	6	1
New York Knicks	46	45	8	4
Oshkosh All-Stars	5	1	3	1
Philadelphia Warriors	51	40		
Providence Steamrollers	5	0		
Rochester/Cincinnati Royals	73	56	15	7
St. Louis Bombers	9	3		
Sheboygan Redskins	6	2		
Syracuse Nationals	39	49	8	5
Toledo Jeeps	5	1		
Tri-Cities/Milwaukee/St. Louis Blackhawks/Hawks	64	57	11	12
Washington Capitols	10	3	4	2
Waterloo Hawks	2	0		
	500	399	75	42

*Does not include Minneapolis-Baltimore games from the 1954–55 season. The Lakers were 3–1 against Baltimore that season, but these games were dropped from official league standings after the Bullets disbanded on November 27, 1954.

1960–61

Western Division	W	L	Pct	GB	Eastern Division	W	L	Pct	GB
St. Louis	51	28	.646	—	Boston	57	22	.722	—
Los Angeles	36	43	.456	15	Philadelphia	46	33	.582	11
Detroit	34	45	.430	17	Syracuse	38	41	.481	19
Cincinnati	33	46	.418	18	New York	21	58	.266	36

NBA Champions–Boston Celtics

1961–62

Western Division	W	L	Pct	GB	Eastern Division	W	L	Pct	GB
Los Angeles	54	26	.675	—	Boston	60	20	.750	—
Cincinnati	43	37	.538	11	Philadelphia	49	31	.613	11
Detroit	37	43	.463	17	Syracuse	41	39	.513	19
St. Louis	29	51	.363	25	New York	29	51	.363	31
Chicago	18	62	.225	36					

NBA Champions–Boston Celtics

1962–63

Western Division	W	L	Pct	GB	Eastern Division	W	L	Pct	GB
Los Angeles	53	27	.663	—	Boston	58	22	.725	—
St. Louis	48	32	.600	5	Syracuse	48	32	.600	10
Detroit	34	46	.425	19	Cincinnati	42	38	.525	16
San Francisco	31	49	.388	22	New York	21	59	.263	37
Chicago	25	55	.313	28					

NBA Champions–Boston Celtics

1963–64

Western Division	W	L	Pct	GB	Eastern Division	W	L	Pct	GB
San Francisco	48	32	.600	—	Boston	59	21	.738	—
St. Louis	46	34	.575	2	Cincinnati	55	25	.688	4
Los Angeles	42	38	.525	6	Philadelphia	34	46	.425	25
Baltimore	31	49	.388	17	New York	22	58	.275	37
Detroit	23	57	.288	25					

NBA Champions–Boston Celtics

1964–65

Western Division	W	L	Pct	GB	Eastern Division	W	L	Pct	GB
Los Angeles	49	31	.613	—	Boston	62	18	.775	—
St. Louis	45	35	.563	4	Cincinnati	48	32	.600	14
Baltimore	37	43	.463	12	Philadelphia	40	40	.500	22
Detroit	31	49	.388	18	New York	31	49	.388	31
San Francisco	17	63	.213	32					

NBA Champions–Boston Celtics

1965–66

Western Division	W	L	Pct	GB	Eastern Division	W	L	Pct	GB
Los Angeles	45	35	.563	—	Philadelphia	55	25	.688	—
Baltimore	38	42	.475	7	Boston	54	26	.675	1
St. Louis	36	44	.450	9	Cincinnati	45	35	.563	10
San Francisco	35	45	.438	10	New York	30	50	.375	23
Detroit	22	58	.275	23					

NBA Champions–Boston Celtics

1966–67

Western Division	W	L	Pct	GB	Eastern Division	W	L	Pct	GB
San Francisco	44	37	.543	—	Philadelphia	68	13	.840	—
St. Louis	39	42	.481	5	Boston	60	21	.741	8
Los Angeles	36	45	.444	8	Cincinnati	39	42	.481	29
Chicago	33	48	.407	11	New York	36	45	.444	32
Detroit	30	51	.370	14	Baltimore	20	61	.247	48

NBA Champions–Philadelphia 76ers

1967-68

Western Division					Eastern Division				
St. Louis	56	26	.683	—	Philadelphia	62	20	.756	—
Los Angeles	52	30	.634	4	Boston	54	28	.659	8
San Francisco	43	39	.524	13	New York	43	39	.524	19
Chicago	29	53	.354	27	Detroit	40	42	.488	22
Seattle	23	59	.280	33	Cincinnati	39	43	.476	23
San Diego	15	67	.183	41	Baltimore	36	46	.439	26

NBA Champions–Boston Celtics

1968-69

Western Division					Eastern Division				
Los Angeles	55	27	.671	—	Baltimore	57	25	.695	—
Atlanta	48	34	.585	7	Philadelphia	55	27	.571	2
San Francisco	41	41	.500	14	New York	54	28	.659	3
San Diego	37	45	.451	18	Boston	48	34	.585	9
Chicago	33	49	.402	22	Cincinnati	41	41	.500	16
Seattle	30	52	.366	25	Detroit	32	50	.390	25
Phoenix	16	66	.195	39	Milwaukee	27	55	.329	30

NBA Champions–Boston Celtics

1969-70

Western Division					Eastern Division				
Atlanta	48	34	.585	—	New York	60	22	.732	—
Los Angeles	46	36	.561	2	Milwaukee	56	26	.683	4
Chicago	39	43	.476	9	Baltimore	50	32	.610	10
Phoenix	39	43	.476	9	Philadelphia	42	40	.512	18
Seattle	36	46	.439	12	Cincinnati	36	46	.439	24
San Francisco	30	52	.366	18	Boston	34	48	.415	26
San Diego	27	55	.329	21	Detroit	31	51	.378	29

NBA Champions–New York Knicks

1970-71

Western Conference

Pacific Division					Midwest Division				
Los Angeles	48	34	.585	—	Milwaukee	66	16	.805	—
San Francisco	41	41	.500	7	Chicago	51	31	.622	15
San Diego	40	42	.488	8	Phoenix	48	34	.585	18
Seattle	38	44	.463	10	Detroit	45	37	.549	21
Portland	29	53	.354	19					

Eastern Conference

Central Division					Atlantic Division				
Baltimore	42	40	.521	—	New York	52	30	.634	—
Atlanta	36	46	.439	6	Philadelphia	47	35	.573	5
Cincinnati	33	49	.402	9	Boston	44	38	.537	8
Cleveland	15	67	.183	27	Buffalo	22	60	.268	30

NBA Champions–Milwaukee Bucks

1971-72

Western Conference

Pacific Division					Midwest Division				
Los Angeles	69	13	.841	—	Milwaukee	63	19	.768	—
Golden State	51	31	.622	18	Chicago	57	25	.695	6
Seattle	47	35	.573	22	Phoenix	49	33	.598	14
Houston	34	48	.415	35	Detroit	26	56	.317	37
Portland	18	64	.220	51					

1971-72

Eastern Conference

Central Division					Atlantic Division				
Baltimore	38	44	.463	—	Boston	56	26	.683	—
Atlanta	36	46	.439	2	New York	48	34	.585	8
Cincinnati	30	52	.366	8	Philadelphia	30	52	.366	26
Cleveland	23	59	.280	15	Buffalo	22	60	.268	34

NBA Champions–Los Angeles Lakers

1972-73

Western Conference

Pacific Division					Midwest Division				
Los Angeles	60	22	.732	—	Milwaukee	60	22	.732	—
Golden State	47	35	.573	13	Chicago	51	31	.622	9
Phoenix	38	44	.463	22	Detroit	40	42	.488	20
Seattle	26	56	.317	34	K.C.-Omaha	36	46	.439	24
Portland	21	61	.256	39					

Eastern Conference

Central Division					Atlantic Division				
Baltimore	52	30	.634	—	Boston	68	14	.829	—
Atlanta	46	36	.561	6	New York	57	25	.695	11
Houston	33	49	.402	19	Buffalo	21	61	.256	47
Cleveland	32	50	.390	20	Philadelphia	9	73	.110	59

NBA Champions–New York Knicks

1973-74

Western Conference

Pacific Division					Midwest Division				
Los Angeles	47	35	.573	—	Milwaukee	59	23	.720	—
Golden State	44	38	.537	3	Chicago	54	28	.659	5
Seattle	36	46	.439	11	Detroit	52	30	.634	7
Phoenix	30	52	.366	17	K.C.-Omaha	33	49	.402	26
Portland	27	55	.329	20					

Eastern Conference

Central Division					Atlantic Division				
Capital	47	35	.573	—	Boston	56	26	.683	—
Atlanta	35	47	.427	12	New York	49	33	.598	7
Houston	32	50	.390	15	Buffalo	42	40	.512	14
Cleveland	29	53	.354	18	Philadelphia	25	57	.305	31

NBA Champions–Boston Celtics

1974-75

Western Conference

Pacific Division					Midwest Division				
Golden State	48	34	.585	—	Chicago	47	35	.573	—
Seattle	43	39	.524	5	K.C.-Omaha	44	38	.537	3
Portland	38	44	.463	10	Detroit	40	42	.488	7
Phoenix	32	50	.390	16	Milwaukee	38	44	.463	9
Los Angeles	30	52	.366	18					

Eastern Conference

Central Division					Atlantic Division				
Washington	60	22	.732	—	Boston	60	22	.732	—
Houston	41	41	.500	19	Buffalo	49	33	.598	11
Cleveland	40	42	.488	20	New York	40	42	.488	20
Atlanta	31	51	.378	29	Philadelphia	34	48	.415	26
New Orleans	23	59	.280	37					

NBA Champions–Golden State Warriors

1975-76

Western Conference

Pacific Division					Midwest Division				
Golden State	59	23	.720	—	Milwaukee	38	44	.463	—
Seattle	43	39	.524	16	Detroit	36	46	.439	2
Phoenix	42	40	.521	17	Kansas City	31	51	.378	7
Los Angeles	40	42	.488	19	Chicago	24	58	.293	14
Portland	37	45	.451	22					

Eastern Conference

Central Division					Atlantic Division				
Cleveland	49	33	.598	—	Boston	54	28	.659	—
Washington	48	34	.585	1	Buffalo	46	36	.561	8
Houston	40	42	.488	9	Philadelphia	46	36	.561	8
New Orleans	38	44	.463	11	New York	38	44	.463	16
Atlanta	29	53	.354	20					

NBA Champions-Boston Celtics

1976-77

Western Conference

Pacific Division					Midwest Division				
Los Angeles	53	29	.646	—	Denver	50	32	.610	—
Portland	49	33	.598	4	Detroit	44	38	.537	6
Golden State	46	36	.561	7	Chicago	44	38	.537	6
Seattle	40	42	.488	13	Kansas City	40	42	.488	10
Phoenix	34	48	.415	19	Indiana	36	46	.439	14
					Milwaukee	30	52	.366	20

Eastern Conference

Central Division					Atlantic Division				
Houston	49	33	.598	—	Philadelphia	50	32	.610	—
Washington	48	34	.585	1	Boston	44	38	.537	6
San Antonio	44	38	.537	5	N.Y. Knicks	40	42	.488	10
Cleveland	43	39	.524	6	Buffalo	30	52	.366	20
New Orleans	35	47	.427	14	N.Y. Nets	22	60	.268	28
Atlanta	31	51	.378	18					

NBA Champions-Portland Trail Blazers

1977-78

Western Conference

Pacific Division					Midwest Division				
Portland	58	24	.707	—	Denver	48	34	.585	—
Phoenix	49	33	.598	9	Milwaukee	44	38	.537	4
Seattle	47	35	.573	11	Chicago	40	42	.488	8
Los Angeles	45	37	.549	13	Detroit	38	44	.463	10
Golden State	43	39	.524	15	Indiana	31	51	.378	17
					Kansas City	31	51	.378	17

Eastern Conference

Central Division					Atlantic Division				
San Antonio	52	30	.634	—	Philadelphia	55	27	.671	—
Washington	44	38	.537	8	New York	43	39	.524	12
Cleveland	43	39	.524	9	Boston	32	50	.390	23
Atlanta	41	41	.500	11	Buffalo	27	55	.329	28
New Orleans	39	43	.476	13	New Jersey	24	58	.293	31
Houston	28	54	.341	24					

NBA Champions-Washington Bullets

1978-79

Western Conference

Pacific Division					Midwest Division				
Seattle	52	30	.634	—	Kansas City	48	34	.585	—
Phoenix	50	32	.610	2	Denver	47	35	.573	1
Los Angeles	47	35	.573	5	Indiana	38	44	.463	10
Portland	45	37	.549	7	Milwaukee	38	44	.463	10
San Diego	43	39	.524	9	Chicago	31	51	.378	17
Golden State	38	44	.463	14					

Eastern Conference

Central Division					Atlantic Division				
San Antonio	48	34	.585	—	Washington	54	28	.659	—
Houston	47	35	.573	1	Philadelphia	47	35	.573	7
Atlanta	46	36	.561	2	New Jersey	37	45	.451	17
Cleveland	30	52	.366	18	New York	31	51	.378	23
Detroit	30	52	.366	18	Boston	29	53	.354	25
New Orleans	26	56	.317	22					

NBA Champions-Seattle Supersonics

1979-80

Western Conference

Pacific Division					Midwest Division				
Los Angeles	60	22	.732	—	Milwaukee	49	33	.598	—
Seattle	56	26	.683	4	Kansas City	47	35	.573	2
Phoenix	55	27	.671	5	Denver	30	52	.366	19
Portland	38	44	.463	22	Chicago	30	52	.366	19
San Diego	35	47	.427	25	Utah	24	58	.293	25
Golden State	24	58	.293	36					

Eastern Conference

Central Division					Atlantic Division				
Atlanta	50	32	.610	—	Boston	61	21	.744	—
Houston	41	41	.500	9	Philadelphia	59	23	.720	2
San Antonio	41	41	.500	9	Washington	39	43	.476	22
Indiana	37	45	.451	13	New York	39	43	.476	22
Cleveland	37	45	.451	13	New Jersey	34	48	.415	27
Detroit	16	66	.195	34					

NBA Champions-Los Angeles Lakers

1980-81

Western Conference

Pacific Division					Midwest Division				
Phoenix	57	25	.695	—	San Antonio	52	30	.634	—
Los Angeles	54	28	.659	3	Kansas City	40	42	.488	12
Portland	45	37	.549	12	Houston	40	42	.488	12
Golden State	39	43	.476	18	Denver	37	45	.451	15
San Diego	36	46	.439	21	Utah	28	54	.341	24
Seattle	34	48	.415	23	Dallas	15	67	.183	37

Eastern Conference

Central Division					Atlantic Division				
Milwaukee	60	22	.732	—	Boston	62	20	.756	—
Chicago	45	37	.549	15	Philadelphia	62	20	.756	—
Indiana	44	38	.537	16	New York	50	32	.610	12
Atlanta	31	51	.378	29	Washington	39	43	.476	23
Cleveland	28	54	.341	32	New Jersey	24	58	.293	38
Detroit	21	61	.256	39					

NBA Champions-Boston Celtics

1981-82

Western Conference

Pacific Division	W	L	Pct	GB	Midwest Division	W	L	Pct	GB
Los Angeles	57	25	.695	—	San Antonio	48	34	.585	—
Seattle	52	30	.634	5	Denver	46	36	.561	2
Phoenix	46	36	.561	11	Houston	46	36	.561	2
Golden State	45	37	.549	12	Kansas City	30	52	.366	18
Portland	42	40	.512	15	Dallas	28	54	.341	20
San Diego	17	65	.207	40	Utah	25	57	.305	23

Eastern Conference

Central Division	W	L	Pct	GB	Atlantic Division	W	L	Pct	GB
Milwaukee	55	27	.671	—	Boston	63	19	.768	—
Atlanta	42	40	.512	13	Philadelphia	58	24	.707	5
Detroit	39	43	.476	16	New Jersey	44	38	.537	19
Indiana	35	47	.427	20	Washington	43	39	.524	20
Chicago	34	48	.415	21	New York	33	49	.402	30
Cleveland	15	67	.183	40					

NBA Champion-Los Angeles Lakers

1982-83

Western Conference

Pacific Division	W	L	Pct	GB	Midwest Division	W	L	Pct	GB
Los Angeles	58	24	.707	—	San Antonio	53	29	.646	—
Phoenix	53	29	.646	5	Denver	45	37	.549	8
Seattle	48	34	.585	10	Kansas City	45	37	.549	8
Portland	46	36	.561	12	Dallas	38	44	.463	15
Golden State	30	52	.366	28	Utah	30	52	.366	23
San Diego	25	57	.305	33	Houston	14	68	.171	39

Eastern Conference

Central Division	W	L	Pct	GB	Atlantic Division	W	L	Pct	GB
Milwaukee	51	31	.622	—	Philadelphia	65	17	.793	—
Atlanta	43	39	.524	8	Boston	56	26	.683	9
Detroit	37	45	.451	14	New Jersey	49	33	.598	16
Chicago	28	54	.341	23	New York	44	38	.537	21
Cleveland	23	59	.280	28	Washington	42	40	.512	23
Indiana	20	62	.244	31					

NBA Champions-Philadelphia 76ers

1983-84

Western Conference

Pacific Division	W	L	Pct	GB	Midwest Division	W	L	Pct	GB
Los Angeles	54	28	.659	—	Utah	45	37	.549	—
Portland	48	34	.585	6	Dallas	43	39	.524	2
Seattle	42	40	.512	12	Denver	38	44	.463	7
Phoenix	41	41	.500	13	Kansas City	38	44	.463	7
Golden State	37	45	.451	17	San Antonio	37	45	.451	8
San Diego	30	52	.366	24	Houston	29	53	.354	16

Eastern Conference

Central Division	W	L	Pct	GB	Atlantic Division	W	L	Pct	GB
Milwaukee	50	32	.610	—	Boston	62	20	.756	—
Detroit	49	33	.598	1	Philadelphia	52	30	.634	10
Atlanta	40	42	.488	10	New York	47	35	.573	15
Cleveland	28	54	.341	22	New Jersey	45	37	.549	17
Chicago	27	55	.329	23	Washington	35	47	.427	27
Indiana	26	56	.317	24					

NBA Champions-Boston Celtics

1984-85

Western Conference

Pacific Division	W	L	Pct	GB	Midwest Division	W	L	Pct	GB
L.A. Lakers	62	20	.756	—	Denver	52	30	.634	—
Portland	42	40	.512	20	Houston	48	34	.585	4
Phoenix	36	46	.439	26	Dallas	44	38	.537	8
L.A. Clippers	31	51	.378	31	San Antonio	41	41	.500	11
Seattle	31	51	.378	31	Utah	41	41	.500	11
Golden State	22	60	.268	40	Kansas City	31	51	.378	21

Eastern Conference

Central Division	W	L	Pct	GB	Atlantic Division	W	L	Pct	GB
Milwaukee	59	23	.720	—	Boston	63	19	.768	—
Detroit	46	36	.561	13	Philadelphia	58	24	.707	5
Chicago	38	44	.463	21	New Jersey	42	40	.512	21
Cleveland	36	46	.439	23	Washington	40	42	.488	23
Atlanta	34	48	.415	25	New York	24	58	.293	39
Indiana	22	60	.268	37					

NBA Champions-Los Angeles Lakers

1985-86

Western Conference

Pacific Division	W	L	Pct	GB	Midwest Division	W	L	Pct	GB
L.A. Lakers	62	20	.756	—	Houston	51	31	.622	—
Portland	40	42	.488	22	Denver	47	35	.573	4
L.A. Clippers	32	50	.390	30	Dallas	44	38	.537	7
Phoenix	32	50	.390	30	Utah	42	40	.512	9
Seattle	31	51	.378	31	Sacramento	37	45	.451	14
Golden State	30	52	.366	32	San Antonio	35	47	.427	16

Eastern Conference

Central Division	W	L	Pct	GB	Atlantic Division	W	L	Pct	GB
Milwaukee	57	25	.695	—	Boston	67	15	.817	—
Atlanta	50	32	.610	7	Philadelphia	54	28	.659	13
Detroit	46	36	.561	11	Washington	39	43	.476	28
Chicago	30	52	.366	27	New Jersey	39	43	.476	28
Cleveland	29	53	.354	28	New York	23	59	.280	44
Indiana	26	56	.317	31					

NBA Champions-Boston Celtics

1986-87

Western Conference

Pacific Division	W	L	Pct	GB	Midwest Division	W	L	Pct	GB
L.A. Lakers	65	17	.793	—	Dallas	55	27	.671	—
Portland	49	33	.598	16	Utah	44	38	.537	11
Golden State	42	40	.512	23	Houston	42	40	.512	13
Seattle	39	43	.476	26	Denver	37	45	.451	18
Phoenix	36	46	.439	29	Sacramento	29	53	.354	26
L.A. Clippers	12	70	.146	53	San Antonio	28	54	.341	27

Eastern Conference

Central Division	W	L	Pct	GB	Atlantic Division	W	L	Pct	GB
Atlanta	57	25	.695	—	Boston	59	23	.720	—
Detroit	52	30	.634	5	Philadelphia	45	37	.549	14
Milwaukee	50	32	.610	7	Washington	42	40	.512	17
Indiana	41	41	.500	16	New Jersey	24	58	.293	35
Chicago	40	42	.488	17	New York	24	58	.293	35
Cleveland	31	51	.378	26					

NBA Champions-Los Angeles Lakers

1987-88

Western Conference

Pacific Division				Midwest Division			
L.A. Lakers	62	20	.756	—	Denver	54 28 .659	—
Portland	53	29	.646	9	Dallas	53 29 .646	1
Seattle	44	38	.537	18	Utah	47 35 .573	7
Phoenix	28	54	.341	34	Houston	46 36 .561	8
Golden State	20	62	.244	42	San Antonio	31 51 .378	23
L.A. Clippers	17	65	.207	45	Sacramento	24 58 .293	30

Eastern Conference

Central Division				Atlantic Division			
Detroit	54	28	.650	—	Boston	57 25 .695	—
Atlanta	50	32	.610	4	Washington	38 44 .463	19
Chicago	50	32	.610	4	New York	38 44 .463	19
Cleveland	42	40	.512	12	Philadelphia	36 46 .439	21
Milwaukee	42	40	.512	12	New Jersey	19 63 .232	38
Indiana	38	44	.463	16			

NBA Champions-Los Angeles Lakers

1988-89

Western Conference

Pacific Division				Midwest Division			
L.A. Lakers	57	25	.695	—	Utah	51 31 .622	—
Phoenix	55	27	.671	2	Houston	45 37 .549	6
Seattle	47	35	.573	10	Denver	44 38 .537	7
Golden State	43	39	.524	14	Dallas	38 44 .463	13
Portland	39	43	.476	18	San Antonio	21 61 .256	30
Sacramento	27	55	.329	30	Miami	15 67 .183	36
L.A. Clippers	21	61	.256	36			

Eastern Conference

Central Division				Atlantic Division			
Detroit	63	19	.768	—	New York	52 30 .634	—
Cleveland	57	25	.695	6	Philadelphia	46 36 .561	6
Atlanta	52	30	.634	11	Boston	42 40 .512	10
Milwaukee	49	33	.598	14	Washington	40 42 .488	12
Chicago	47	35	.573	16	New Jersey	26 56 .317	26
Indiana	28	54	.341	35	Charlotte	20 62 .244	32

NBA Champions–Detroit Pistons

Los Angeles Lakers Record Vs.

	Regular Season		Playoffs	
	W	L	W	L
Boston Celtics	59	82	25	32
Buffalo Braves; San Diego/ Los Angeles Clippers	72	24		
Charlotte Hornets	2	0		
Chicago Bulls	58	39	16	7
Chicago Packers/Zephyrs; Baltimore/Capital/Washington Bullets	84	52	4	2
Cincinnati Royals; Kansas City-Omaha/Kansas City/ Sacramento Kings	127	58	3	0
Cleveland Cavaliers	38	18		
Dallas Mavericks	32	12	12	6
Denver Nuggets	38	24	9	2
Detroit Pistons	105	55	11	11
Indiana Pacers	27	5		
Miami Heat	4	0		
Milwaukee Bucks	47	32	6	10
New York Knicks	89	50	8	9
New York/New Jersey Nets	25	7		
New Orleans/Utah Jazz	52	16	4	3
Philadelphia/San Francisco/ Golden State Warriors	123	81	20	10
Phoenix Suns	75	49	23	6
Portland Trail Blazers	72	36	11	6
San Antonio Spurs	35	23	14	2
San Diego/Houston Rockets	80	27	2	6
Seattle Supersonics	86	45	14	7
St. Louis/Atlanta Hawks	91	67	21	14
Syracuse Nationals/ Philadelphia 76ers	77	64	8	8
	1498	866	211	141

Yearly Team Leaders

	Scoring Avg.	Rebounds/Game	Assists/Game		Minutes/Game	Field Goal Pct.	Free Throw Pct.
1947–48	Mikan 21.3			1947–48			Schaefer .800
1948–49	Mikan 28.3		Mikan 3.6	1948–49		Mikan .416	Schaefer .817
1949–50	Mikan 27.4		Pollard 3.8	1949–50		Mikan .407	Schaefer .851
1950–51	Mikan 28.4	Mikan 14.1	Martin 3.5	1950–51		Mikan .428	Mikan .803
1951–52	Mikan 23.8	Mikan 13.5	Martin 3.8	1951–52	Mikan 40.2	Mikkelsen .419	Mikan .780
1952–53	Mikan 20.6	Mikan 14.4	Martin 3.6	1952–53	Mikan 37.9	Mikkelsen .435	Martin .780
1953–54	Mikan 18.1	Mikan 14.3	Martin 3.7	1953–54	Pollard 35.0	Lovellette .423	Pollard .778
1954–55	Lovellette 18.7	Lovellette 11.5	Martin 5.9	1954–55	Martin 38.7	Lovellette .435	Schnittker .823
1955–56	Lovellette 21.5	Lovellette 14.0	Martin 6.2	1955–56	Martin 39.4	Lovellette .434	Schnittker .856
1956–57	Lovellette 20.8	Lovellette 13.5	Mencel 2.8	1956–57	Lovellette 36.1	Lovellette .426	Garmaker .839
1957–58	Mikkelsen 17.3	Foust 12.2	Leonard 3.3	1957–58	Mikkelsen 33.2	Mikkelsen .410	Schnittker .848
1958–59	Baylor 24.9	Baylor 15.0	Baylor 4.1	1958–59	Baylor 40.8	Baylor .408	Mikkelsen .806
1959–60	Baylor 29.6	Baylor 16.4	Hundley 4.6	1959–60	Baylor 41.0	Baylor .424	Hundley .744
1960–61	Baylor 34.8	Baylor 19.8	Baylor 5.1	1960–61	Baylor 42.9	Hawkins .431	LaRusso .790
1961–62	West 30.8	Baylor 18.6	West 5.4	1961–62	West 41.2	LaRusso .466	West .769
1962–63	Baylor 34.0	Baylor 14.3	Baylor 4.8	1962–63	Baylor 42.1	Barnett .471	Baylor .837
1963–64	West 28.7	Baylor 12.0	West 5.6	1963–64	Baylor 40.6	West .484	West .832
1964–65	West 31.0	Baylor 12.8	West 4.9	1964–65	West 41.4	West .497	West .821
1965–66	West 31.3	Ellis 9.2	West 6.1	1965–66	West 40.7	Boozer .484	West .860
1966–67	West 28.7	Imhoff 13.3	West 6.8	1966–67	Imhoff 33.6	Hawkins .481	West .878
1967–68	Baylor 26.0	Baylor 12.2	Baylor 4.6	1967–68	Clark 37.5	West .514	West .811
1968–69	Baylor 24.8	Chamberlain 21.1	West 6.9	1968–69	Chamberlain 45.3	Chamberlain .538	Egan .850
1969–70	West 31.2	Hairston 12.2	West 7.5	1969–70	West 42.0	West .497	West .824
1970–71	West 26.9	Chamberlain 18.2	West 9.5	1970–71	Chamberlain 44.3	Chamberlain .545	West .832
1971–72	Goodrich 25.9	Chamberlain 19.2	West 9.7	1971–72	Chamberlain 42.3	Chamberlain .649	Goodrich .850
1972–73	Goodrich 23.9	Chamberlain 18.6	West 8.8	1972–73	Chamberlain 43.2	Chamberlain .727	McMillian .845
1973–74	Goodrich 25.3	Hairston 13.5	Goodrich 5.2	1973–74	Goodrich 37.3	Hairston .507	Goodrich .864
1974–75	Goodrich 22.6	Hairston 12.8	Goodrich 5.8	1974–75	Goodrich 37.1	Hairston .506	Goodrich .841
1975–76	Abdul-Jabbar 27.7	Abdul-Jabbar 16.9	Goodrich 5.6	1975–76	Abdul-Jabbar 41.2	Abdul-Jabbar .529	Russell .892
1976–77	Abdul-Jabbar 26.2	Abdul-Jabbar 13.3	Allen 5.2	1976–77	Abdul-Jabbar 36.8	Abdul-Jabbar .579	Russell .858
1977–78	Abdul-Jabbar 25.8	Abdul-Jabbar 12.9	Nixon 6.8	1977–78	Nixon 34.3	Abdul-Jabbar .550	Dantley .801
1978–79	Abdul-Jabbar 23.8	Abdul-Jabbar 12.8	Nixon 9.0	1978–79	Abdul-Jabbar 39.5	Abdul-Jabbar .577	Dantley .854
1979–80	Abdul-Jabbar 24.8	Abdul-Jabbar 10.8	Nixon 7.8	1979–80	Nixon 39.3	Abdul-Jabbar .604	Johnson .810
1980–81	Abdul-Jabbar 26.2	Abdul-Jabbar 10.3	Nixon 8.8	1980–81	Wilkes 37.4	Abdul-Jabbar .574	Nixon .778
1981–82	Abdul-Jabbar 23.9	Johnson 9.6	Nixon 8.0	1981–82	Johnson 38.4	Abdul-Jabbar .579	Cooper .813
1982–83	Abdul-Jabbar 21.8	Johnson 8.6	Johnson 10.5	1982–83	Johnson 36.8	Abdul-Jabbar .588	Johnson .800
1983–84	Abdul-Jabbar 21.5	Abdul-Jabbar 7.3	Johnson 13.1	1983–84	Johnson 38.3	McGee .594	Cooper .838
1984–85	Abdul-Jabbar 22.0	Abdul-Jabbar 7.9	Johnson 12.6	1984–85	Johnson 36.1	Abdul-Jabbar .599	Johnson .843
1985–86	Abdul-Jabbar 23.4	Lucas 7.4	Johnson 12.6	1985–86	Johnson 35.8	Worthy .579	Johnson .871
1986–87	Johnson 23.9	Green 7.8	Johnson 12.2	1986–87	Johnson 36.3	Abdul-Jabbar .564	Scott .892
1987–88	Scott 21.7	Green 8.7	Johnson 11.9	1987–88	Scott 37.6	Abdul-Jabbar .532	Scott .858
1988–89	Johnson 22.5	Green 9.0	Johnson 12.8	1988–89	Johnson 37.5	Worthy .548	Johnson .911

Underline indicates league leadership for that year

LAKERS ALL-TIME CAREER LEADERS

GAMES PLAYED		POINTS	
Kareem Abdul-Jabbar	1,093	Jerry West	25,192
Jerry West	932	Kareem Abdul-Jabbar	24,176
Elgin Baylor	846	Elgin Baylor	23,149
Michael Cooper	793	Magic Johnson	13,943
Magic Johnson	716	Gail Goodrich	13,044
Vern Mikkelsen	699	George Mikan	11,351
Gail Goodrich	687	Jamaal Wilkes	10,601
Rudy LaRusso	583	Vern Mikkelsen	10,063
Jamaal Wilkes	575	James Worthy	9,857
James Worthy	552	Rudy LaRusso	8,231

SCORING AVERAGE		REBOUNDING AVERAGE	
Elgin Baylor	27.4	Wilt Chamberlain	19.2
Jerry West	27.0	Elgin Baylor	13.5
George Mikan	22.9	George Mikan	13.4
Kareem Abdul-Jabbar	22.1	Happy Hairston	12.4
Magic Johnson	19.5	Clyde Lovellette	11.1
Gail Goodrich	19.0	Elmore Smith	11.1
Jamaal Wilkes	18.4	Darrall Imhoff	9.4
Adrian Dantley	18.3	Vern Mikkelsen	9.4
James Worthy	17.9	Kareem Abdul-Jabbar	9.4
Wilt Chamberlain	17.7	Rudy LaRusso	9.3

Minneapolis Lakers vs. Harlem Globetrotters

February 19, 1948 at Chicago Stadium. Attendance–17,823.
Globetrotters 61, Lakers 59

February 28, 1949 at Chicago Stadium. Attendance–20,046.
Globetrotters 49, Lakers 45

March 14, 1949 at Minneapolis Auditorium. Attendance–10,122.
Lakers 68, Globetrotters 53

February 21, 1950 at Chicago Stadium. Attendance–21,666.
Lakers 76, Globetrotters 60

March 20, 1950 at St. Paul Auditorium. Attendance–9,807.
Lakers 69, Globetrotters 54

February 23, 1951 at Chicago Stadium. Attendance–16,963.
Lakers 72, Globetrotters 68

January 2, 1952 at Chicago Stadium. Attendance–20,004.
Lakers 84, Globetrotters 60

January 3, 1958 at Chicago Stadium. Attendance–11,033.
Lakers 111, Globetrotters 100

Los Angeles Lakers Games Played in Minneapolis
All games at the Minneapolis Auditorium

Sunday, December 17, 1961. Attendance–6,213.
Lakers 122, Detroit Pistons 116
Jerry West 47 points

Sunday, December 9, 1962. Attendance–7,612.
Syracuse Nationals 117, Lakers 114
Elgin Baylor 34 points

Monday, November 11, 1963. Attendance–7,822.
Detroit Pistons 116, Lakers 109
Elgin Baylor 28 points

Sunday, December 6, 1964. Attendance–8,007.
Lakers 109, Philadelphia 76ers 104
Jerry West 30 points

Friday, November 12, 1965. Attendance–8,690.
Lakers 107, New York Knicks 106.
Jerry West 29 points

Lakers in Naismith Memorial Hall of Fame
(Years with team in parentheses)

	Year of Induction
George Mikan (Player 1947-54, 1956; Coach 1957-58)	1959
Bill Sharman (Coach 1971-76)	1975
Elgin Baylor (1958-72)	1976
Jim Pollard (Player 1947-55; Coach 1960)	1977
Wilt Chamberlain (1968-73)	1978
Jerry West (Player 1960-74; Coach 1976-79)	1979
Slater Martin (1949-56)	1981
Clyde Lovellette (1953-57)	1988

THE ORIGINAL LAKERS

Warren Ajax	Paul Napolitano
Don (Swede) Carlson	Joe Patanelli
Bill Durkee	Jim Pollard
Ken Exel	Jack Rocker
Bob Gerber	Don Smith
Tony Jaros	

BIBLIOGRAPHY

Library files of the *Chicago Tribune, Los Angeles Examiner, Los Angeles Times, Minneapolis Star, Minneapolis Tribune, New York Times, St. Paul Dispatch, St. Paul Pioneer Press.*

Abdul-Jabbar, Kareem. *Giant Steps.* New York: Bantam House, 1982.

Carlson, Stan W. *The Minneapolis Lakers: World Champions of Professional Basketball.* Minneapolis: The Olympic Press, 1950.

Chamberlain, Wilt. *Wilt.* New York: Warner Paperback Library, 1973.

Devaney, John. *The Story of Basketball.* New York: Random House, 1976.

Dickey, Glenn. *The History of Professional Basketball Since 1896.* New York: Stein and Day, 1982.

Dolan, Jr., Edward F. *Great Moments in the NBA Championships.* New York: Franklin Watts, 1982.

Gutman, Bill. *The Pictoral History of Basketball.* New York: Gallery Books, 1988.

Harris, Merv. *The Fabulous Lakers.* New York: Lancer Books, 1972.

Harris, Merv. *The Lonely Heroes.* New York: The Viking Press, 1975.

Hill, Bob, and Baron, Randall. *The Amazing Basketball Book: The First 100 Years.* Louisville: Full Court Press, 1987.

Hoffman, Anne Byrne. *Echoes From the Schoolyard: Informal Portraits of NBA Greats.* New York: Hawthorn Books, Inc., 1977.

Hollander, Zander, ed. *The Modern Encyclopedia of Basketball.* Garden City, NY: Dolphin Books, 1979.

Hollander, Zander, ed. *The Pro Basketball Encyclopedia.* Los Angeles: Corwin Books, 1977.

Isaacs, Neil. *All the Moves: A History of College Basketball.* Philadelphia: J. B. Lippincott Company, 1975.

Jares, Joe. *Basketball: The American Game.* Chicago: Follett Publishing Co., 1971.

Koppett, Leonard. *Championship NBA.* New York: The Dial Press, 1970.

Koppett, Leonard. *24 Seconds to Shoot: An Informal History of the National Basketball Association.* New York: The Macmillan Company, 1968.

Krenz, Joel B. *Gopher State Greatness.* Minneapolis: Richtman's Printing, 1984.

Krishef, Robert K. *Thank You, America: The Biography of Benjamin N. Berger.* Minneapolis: Dillon Press, Inc., 1982.

Libby, Bill. *Goliath: The Wilt Chamberlain Story.* New York: Dodd, Mead & Company, 1977.

Liss, Howard. *Strange But True Basketball Stories.* New York: Random House, 1972.

McCallum, John D. *College Basketball, U.S.A. Since 1892.* New York: Stein and Day, 1978.

McGrane, Bill. *Bud: The Other Side of the Glacier.* New York: Harper & Row, 1986.

Mendell, Ronald L. *Who's Who in Basketball.* New Rochelle, NY: Arlington House, 1973.

Menke, Frank G. *The Encyclopedia of Sports.* New York: A. S. Barnes and Company, 1975.

Menville, Chuck. *The Harlem Globetrotters: Fifty Years of Fun and Games.* New York: David McKay Company, Inc., 1978.

Mikan, George. *Mr. Basketball: George Mikan's Own Story.* New York: Greenberg, 1951.

NBA Guide. St. Louis: The Sporting News, 1987.

NBA . . . 25 Actions Years. Revere, MA: Fleetwood Recording Company, Inc., 1971.

Ostler, Scott, and Springer, Steve. *Winnin' Times: The Magical Journey of the Los Angeles Lakers.* New York: Macmillan, 1986.

Packer, Billy. *50 Years of the Final Four.* Dallas: Taylor Publishing, 1987.

Padwe, Sandy. *Basketball's Hall of Fame.* Englewood Cliffs, NJ: Prentice-Hall, 1978.

Rappoport, Ken. *The Classic: The History of the NCAA Basketball Championship.* Mission, KS: NCAA, 1979.

Riley, Pat. *Showtime: Inside the Lakers' Breakthrough Season.* New York: Warner Books, Inc., 1988.

Rosen, Charles. *God, Man and Basketball Jones.* New York: Holt, Rinehart and Winston, 1979.

Russell, Bill. *Go Up for Glory.* New York: Coward-McCann, Inc., 1966.

Russell, Bill, and Branch, Taylor. *Second Wind: The Memoirs of an Opinionated Man.* New York: Random House, 1979.

Sabin, Lou. *Great Teams of Pro Basketball.* New York: Random House, 1971.

Salzberg, Charles. *From Set Shot to Slam Dunk.* New York: E. P. Dutton, 1987.

Shecter, Leonard. *The Jocks.* New York: Warner Paperback Library, 1969.

Stern, Robert. *They Were Number One: A History of the NCAA Basketball Tournament.* New York: Leisure Press, 1983.

Sullivan, George. *The Picture History of the Boston Celtics.* New York: The Bobbs-Merrill Company, Inc., 1981.

Sullivan, Neil J. *The Dodgers Move West.* New York: Oxford University Press, 1987.

Vescey, George, ed. *The Way It Was.* New York McGraw-Hill, 1974.

Wallechinsky, David. *The Complete Book of the Olympics.* New York: Penguin Books, 1984.

West, Jerry. *Mr. Clutch: The Jerry West Story.* New York: Grosset & Dunlap, 1971.

Weyand, Alexander M. *The Cavalcade of Basketball.* New York: The Macmillan Company, 1960.

Wilson, Kenneth L. (Tug), and Brondfield, Jerry. *The Big Ten.* Englewood Cliffs, NJ: Prentice-Hall, Inc., 1967.

PHOTO CREDITS

Index

118